АГ552794

Frantz Fanon

Frantz Fanon
Colonialism and Alienation

Concerning Frantz Fanon's Political Theory

Renate Zahar

Translated by
Willfried F. Feuser

AAKAR

Frantz Fanon
Renate Zahar

© Monthly Review Press 1974
© Aakar Books for South Asia 2010

First Published in India, 2010
Reprinted 2025

ISBN 978-93-5002-040-1 (Pb)

Published in agreement with Monthly Review Press, New York for publication and sale only in South Asia.

All rights reserved. No part of this book may be reproduced or transmitted, in any form or by any means, without prior permission of the publisher.

Published by
AAKAR BOOKS
28 E Pocket IV, Mayur Vihar Phase I
Delhi 110 091, India
www.aakarbooks.com

Printed at
D.K. Fine Art Press, Delhi

Contents

Biographical Sketch*

As Fanon's political activity had a considerable bearing on the development of his theory, just as his theory was constantly geared to revolutionary practice, it is appropriate first of all to outline his life and activity.

Frantz Fanon was born in Fort-de-France, the capital of the French colony of Martinique, on 20 July 1925. He was a black man, the descendant of slaves carried off from Africa to the Antilles. Despite the racial discrimination to which they were subjected, the situation of these Negroes differed from that of the blacks in the African colonies. In the Antilles a black bourgeoisie had already evolved which strove for assimilation rather than national independence. Fanon's family belonged to this class. His father (1891–1947) was a customs inspector; five of the eight children after finishing secondary school went on to study in French universities.

The events of the Second World War in 1941 had their repercussions even on the remote island of Martinique. Under the pressure of the American blockade the French Governor Robert, a partisan of the Vichy régime, established a military dictatorship, which was supported by the handful of propertied families dominant in Martinique. In this situation Fanon conceived of a plan to leave the island in order to join the Allied forces. Personal and family reasons played a part in

* The data on Frantz Fanon's life and activity used here are mostly owed to the research of Giovanni Pirelli, whom I would like to thank for his cooperation.

this decision; Fanon's political motives were not clear-cut, for wasn't this war a conflict between whites, whereas the struggle of the Martiniquans ought to have had as its objective the emancipation from the whites, i.e., the struggle against all whites? At the end of 1943, when Fanon had made up his mind to fight on the Allied side and fled to Dominica to join the British, the first local demonstrations were developing against the French colonizers. Under the pressure of the American blockade the government of Martinique rallied to de Gaulle. Fanon returned, was drafted into the army and left Fort-de-France in 1944 for North Africa. At Bougie near Constantine he attended an officers' training course. This brief stay was his first contact with Algeria, which was later to become his adopted country. He was wounded in action near the Swiss border and awarded a decoration for bravery; the accompanying document bore the signature of Colonel Raoul Salan, the same man who in 1956 was to become the supreme commander of the French army in Algeria and later the leader of the Organisation de l'Armée Secrète. Fanon saw the end of the war in Germany. After his discharge from the army he returned to Martinique just in time to support the election campaign of Aimé Césaire, the Communist Party candidate for the first National Assembly of the IVth Republic, together with his brother Joby.[1] This was his first specifically political experience.

---

[1] At this period and for some years to come Césaire's personailty exerted a strong influence on the young Fanon. Fanon had made Césaire's acquaintance during his last year in high school, when Césaire was his French teacher. This early link was still very much in evidence in his first book, *Black Skin, White Masks*. In his essay, 'West Indians and Africans', published in 1955 he wrote: 'For the first time a *lycée* teacher —a man, therefore, who was apparently worthy of respect—was seen to announce quite simply to West Indian society "that it is fine and good to be a Negro." To be sure this created a scandal...Two centuries of white truth proved this man to be wrong. He must be mad, for it was unthinkable that he could be right.' Frantz Fanon, *Toward the African Revolution*, trans. Haakon Chevalier (New York: Monthly Review Press, 1967), pp. 21–22.

After his baccalaureate examination in March 1946 the wounded and decorated war veteran obtained a scholarship. He registered in the medical faculty at Lyons. These first years of direct contact with European culture were divided between two poles of attraction: on the one hand, medicine, on the other, philosophy and literature. He attended the lectures of Jean Lacroix and Maurice Merleau-Pontry and read Kierkegaard and Nietzsche, Hegel, Marx and Lenin, Husserl, Heidegger and Sartre. During his first years at university he wrote some plays which remained unpublished. Later he turned especially to neuropsychiatry and neurosurgery since these subjects best answered his need for humanist commitment. His attention was then increasingly focussed on political problems; at Lyons he studied extensively the conditions under which the North African immigrants in France were living.[1]

Subsequently, however, the political differences between Fanon and Césaire increased, leading to a break in their relations when in 1958 Césaire called upon the Martiniquans to vote *Yes* in de Gaulle's referendum.

In late 1951 he concluded his studies with a dissertation on 'A Case of Friedreich's Disease' and for the last time returned to Martinique. Back in France he worked in the clinic of Saint Alban de Losère, together with the Spanish emigrant, Dr Tosquelle, to whom, according to his own testimony, he owed a great deal in the field of social therapy.

In October 1952, Fanon married Marie-Josèphe ('Josie') Dublé, a French girl he had known since he studied in Lyons. At that time he had already made up his mind to work in Africa for a few years and then

[1] In 1952 he published an article in *Esprit*, 'Le Syndrome nord-africain', in which he analyzed the specific psychic disturbances of North African immigrants whom he met in his medical practice. See The "North African Syndrome" in Fanon, *Toward the African Revolution*, pp. 3–16.

to return to Martinique. Since a letter addressed to Senghor, in which he had asked for a job in an African hospital, remained unanswered, he accepted the offer of the French Governor General in Algeria, Robert Lacoste, to become *chef de service* at the Blida-Joinville psychiatric clinic. His activity as a psychiatrist in this hospital was to last barely three years, from November 1953 to January 1957. According to his friends those were happy years; his experiences at Blida were in complete harmony with his interests, and his political awareness was sharpened by the revolutionary situation of the incipient liberation struggle.

At Blida, the most important psychiatric hospital on African soil, Fanon took over a ward with 165 European women and 220 Algerian men. He now had an opportunity of applying the techniques of social therapy which he had elaborated together with Tosquelle. In his treatment he tried to develop new forms of corporate life infused with a democratic spirit in order to put in motion processes of socialization which should enable the patients to find their bearings in society again. He endeavoured to establish a close link between pyschotherapy and political education. But when trying to apply methods that had been geared to Europeans to his Arab patients, he ran into insurmountable obstacles resulting from the fact that the social conditions under which the patients were accustomed to living had not been taken into account in prescribing the therapy.[1] The contradictions he met when applying treatment could only be understood in political categories.

---

[1] These experiences have been described at length by a colleague of Fanon's. See Jack Azoulay, 'Contribution à l'Etude de la Socialthérapie dans un Service d'Aliénés musulmans', (University of Algiers, Faculty of Medicine 1954). Also the article by Azoulay and Fanon: 'La Socialthérapie dans un Service d'Hommes musulmans" in *L'Information Psychiatrique*, 9, Paris (1954).

> Madness is one of the means man has of losing his freedom. And I can say, on the basis of what I have been able to observe from this point of vantage, that the degree of alienation of the inhabitants of this country is frightening. If psychiatry is the medical technique that aims to enable man no longer to be a stranger to his environment, I owe it to myself that the Arab, permanently an alien in his own country, lives in a state of absolute depersonalization.[1]

Thus Fanon wrote in his letter of resignation addressed to Lacoste in 1956.

Fanon's revolutionary commitment originated from the logic inherent in his professional practice and was increasingly radicalized through his personal experience of the Algerian liberation struggle. It is impossible to ascertain when precisely his concrete collaboration with the Algerian Liberation Front started, whether in his encounters with the revolutionary leaders of the underground, such as Abane Ramdane, or through contacts with the *Armée de Libération Nationale* (*ALN*), which was operating in the vicinity of Blida. Fanon was in a favourable position for any underground activity; he hid members of the *Front de Libération Nationale* (*FLN*), trained nurses for the underground struggle, offered rooms for secret meetings, and relayed information, arms and other material. He played a leading part in the setting up and training of commando units and taught the *moujahedin* how to lay booby-traps, how to control their reflexes when making bomb attempts, and which mental or physical attitude to adopt in order to endure tortures. The underground organization of the hospital was discovered in late 1956. Some members fled, others were sent to a concentration camp or deported from the country, like Fanon himself. Since in the previous summer he had already written a strongly-worded and politically unambiguous letter of resignation and

[1] Fanon. *Toward the African Revolution*, p. 53.

in September had proclaimed the necessity of the war of liberation before a congress of black writers and artists, he probably owed this relatively harmless sanction on the part of the French administration to his aura as a humanist intellectual. After a brief clandestine sojourn in Paris he went to Tunisia via Switzerland and Italy.

In Tunisia, where his wife and son joined him, he immediately resumed his dual activity. He worked both at La Manouba, the psychiatric hospital of Tunis, changing to the psychiatric ward of the Charles Nicolle Policlinic in the summer of 1958, and in the editorial office of *Résistance Algérienne*, the organ of both the National Liberation Army and the National Liberation Front, starting immediately after his arrival. In addition he lectured at the University of Tunis. It was the period when the *Comité de Coordination et d'Exécution* (*CCE*), which had been formed after the Soummam Congress in 1956 and was superseded by the *Provisional Government of the Algerian Republic* (*GPRA*) as from September 1958, was concentrating the major part of its activity in the Tunisian capital. In the summer Fanon was summoned to Tetuan, where the reorganization of the entire FLN press was discussed. After his return began a period of close collaboration with the editorial board of *El Moudjahid*, where he helped to shape the political orientation of the FLN, both at the internal and the international levels.

The death of Abane Ramdane, murdered by Algerians on the Algerian-Moroccan border in early 1958, must have been a serious shock to Fanon, his friend and political comrade-in-arms especially since, as a member of the editorial staff of *El Moudjahid*, he had to subscribe to a falsified official version of his death. The essays published under the title *Year V of the Algerian Revolution*, which he wrote shortly afterwards were among other things an expression of his need to objectify the motives of the liberation struggle transcending the revolutionary's personal conflict between his individual political commitment and the demands of revolutionary discipline, and to probe the emancipatory processes among the colonial population triggered off by the revolution.

In December 1958 Fanon spoke for the first time before a Pan-African Congress in Accra as a member of the Algerian delegation. Here he met Nkrumah, the president of an already-independent Ghana, Lumumba, who together with Diomi and Ngalula represented the Mouvement National Congolais (MNC), Felix Moumié, the leader of the Union Populaire du Cameroun (UPC), Tom M'Boya, the Secretary of the Kenyan trade union and leader of the Kenya Independence Movement, as well as Roberto Holden, who later was to become the leader of the União das Populações de Angola (UPA). For Fanon, the political perspectives of integrating the Algerian revolution into the Pan-African liberation struggle assumed concrete form in such contacts, and this in turn conditioned the outlook of Fanon the theoretician and future author of *The Wretched of the Earth*.

Some months later Fanon spoke once more at an international conference, the Second Congress of Black Writers and Artists, which took place in Rome, 26–31 March 1959. He spoke as a member of the West Indian delegation.

In the summer of the same year he was seriously injured in a traffic accident near the Algerian-Moroccan border, where he was reorganizing the medical services of the military sector and training the ALN cadres. First he was reported dead in Tunisia, then, more dead than alive, he was flown to Rome, where he spent several months in a hospital. During this period the 'Red Hand'* made two attempts on Fanon's life.

---

* La 'Main Rouge' was a French right-wing terrorist organization responsible, among other things, for the murder of Félix Moumié, in 1960. (Trans. note).

A time bomb at Rome airport exploded prematurely, killing two children; the nocturnal commando of assassins which penetrated into the hospital found his bed empty as his suspicions had been aroused and he had insisted on being transferred to another room that very evening. After a brief spell of convalescence he returned to Tunis at the end of 1959.

Nineteen-sixty was a year of crucial importance for Africa. Many colonies obtained their political independence. Their future relations with the former colonial powers but also with the two main centres of industrial development, as well as the relations of the newly independent states with each other and their support for the various national liberation struggles began to crystallize in the discussions on the so-called 'African Socialism'. In January Fanon took part in the second conference of African peoples held in Tunis, this time as a member of the Algerian delegation. The changes which had occurred since the first conference at Accra were discussed. The spokesman of the Algerian delegation called for the formation of an international brigade of African volunteers for the struggle against French colonialism.

The following month Fanon appeared in Cairo, the seat of the GPRA's Ministry of Foreign Affairs, in his new capacity as the permanent representative of the Provisional Algerian Government in Accra to discuss the guidelines of an African policy. At that time Accra was the centre of contacts and discussions for progressive African politicians and revolutionaries. As the representative of a country which for six years had been waging a bitter struggle for independence, Fanon enjoyed particular prestige. Here was the committed revolutionary incarnate, the French intellectual who had broken with the motherland to fight in the frontline of the anti-imperialist struggle; here was the black man, the descendant of slaves deported from the continent, who had returned as a militant and as the theoretician of African independence. He symbolized both the link between the two traditional Africas north and south of the Sahara and the internationalism of the 'Third World', which previously tended to be bogged down in non-committal and purely propagandistic formulations but was now becoming an absolute necessity.

Henceforth Fanon appeared as the official diplomatic representative of Algeria at international congresses (Conference for Peace and Security, Accra, 7–10 April; Afro-Asian Conference, Conakry, 12–15 April; Third Conference of Independent African States, Addis Ababa, June 1960). This gave greater weight to his political stance and his contacts with other African politicians. His main concern was to herald the Algerian struggle as a lodestar and an example for the whole of Africa and at the same time to drive home to the Algerians their relationship with Africa in political terms. Using this angle as his starting point, he focussed his attention on three problems of acute interest: the establishment of the southern front along the Malian border, the beginning of the armed struggle in Angola, and the events in the Congo.

His project to import arms and ammunition from Mali and to mobilize the population of the Sahara more strongly for the struggle took on concrete forms during Fanon's second visit to Mali; the plan in its general outlines was approved by the GPRA, and direct negotiations were conducted with Modibo Keita, the president of Mali. However, the project never reached fruition. Shortly after his second visit to Mali, Fanon was forced to remain in Tunis because his health deteriorated, and he was never to return to Black Africa again.

In Angola, where the tensions between the colonized and the colonizers had reached crisis point, Fanon saw the possibility of creating 'a second Algeria', preferably while the Algerian war was still going on and the tensions in the Congo kept increasing. Fanon supported and advised Roberto Holden, whom he had known since 1959.[1] He obtained the support of other African leaders for him; he managed to bring him and his UPA partisans to Tunis, where in close collaboration with the ALN and with the tacit consent of the Tunisian government, they were given training in the techniques of guerrilla warfare. During the very months that Fanon was active in Accra, the offensive of Belgian colonialism and international capital in the Congo began to appear in outline. In June 1960 the Congo obtained its independence; Lumumba became prime minister; only a few weeks later Tshombe proclaimed Katanga's independence; Belgian troops stepped in, and in September the UNO intervened. It is true that Fanon did not exert any direct influence on the events taking place in the Congo in those months; on the other hand, it is correct to speak of a definite interaction of Fanon's and Lumumba's political and strategic thinking. After their first encounter in Accra, in December 1958, they met again several times, both in Accra and in what was then Léopoldville, the meeting place of the Pan-African Conference summoned by Lumumba at the height of the Katangan secession, in August 1960. In September 1960, Lumumba was arrested illegally; the UNO, invoking the principle of non-intervention, refused to save the representative of the central government elected by the people, and in January 1961 he was murdered.

---

[1] Fanon supported Holden and his movement throughout his life even at a time when it could already seriously be argued that the latter was an agent of the United States. At the same time he refused to consider the Movimento Popular de Libertação de Angola (Angolan People's Liberation Movement) (APLM) and its leader, Agostinho Neto, representative, and as such to accord them recognition. Apart from the personal motive of his friendship with Roberto Holden he may have opted for the UPA, as the peasant movement, in preference to the MPLA, which had originated from the experience of the urban struggle, especially in Luanda.

Fanon analyzed these events as being typical of imperialist policy in Africa. They led to a great deal of soul-searching on his part and prompted him to address the following appeal to all progressive African politicians:

> Africa must understand . . . that there will not be one Africa that fights against colonialism and another that attempts to make arrangements with colonialism . . . Our mistake, the mistake we Africans made, was to have forgotten that the enemy never withdraws sincerely. He never understands. He capitulates, but he does not become converted. Our mistake is to have believed that the enemy had lost his combativeness and his harmfulness. If Lumumba is in the way, Lumumba disappears. Hesitation in murder has never characterized imperialism. Look at Ben M'hidi, look at Moumié, look at Lumumba. Our mistake is to have been slightly confused in what we did. It is a fact that in Africa, today, traitors exist. They should have been denounced and fought. The fact that this is hard after the magnificent dream of an Africa gathered together unto itself and subject to the same requirements of true independence does not alter facts . . . Let us be sure never to forget it: the fate of us all is at stake in the Congo.[1]

Probably Fanon already knew about his disease while in Accra; during his stay in Tunis in December 1960 he learned with absolute certainty that he was suffering from leukemia and had at most a few years but possibly only a few months to live. The doctors in a Moscow hospital, where he spent a few weeks, advised him to go to the United States for special treatment and at any rate to look after his health and not to leave the hospital. Thereupon Fanon returned to Algeria at once and requested the GPRA to send him to Cuba as its permanent representative. Under the given circumstances, this request was as characteristic of him as the fact that during the next few months he

---

[1] Fanon, 'Lumumba's death: Could we do otherwise?' in *African Revolution*, pp. 192–197.

was to be found in the vicinity of Gardimaou on the Tunisian-Algerian border giving political training courses to ALN cadres.[1]

He attached great importance to this work, which used up whatever little energy was left in him. The end of the war was in sight; it was now a matter of developing the consciousness of the future avant-garde along the lines of the awakening of consciousness he had analysed in *L'An V de la Révolution Algérienne*. Some time later, Fanon's stay with the cadres of the 'Frontier Army' was to give Ben Bella occasion for presenting himself, together with Boumedienne, as the heir of Fanon's ideas and the proponent of progressive socialist thinking when he broke away from the GPRA.

In April Fanon began writing on borrowed time; his health was visibly deteriorating. After about ten weeks he sent the last chapter of *The Wretched of the Earth* to his publisher. 'I am under the impression' he wrote, 'that I have been very, or even too vehement in my descriptions. The reason is that I feel the whole project is at stake.'

In August he met Sartre for a few days in Rome. He asked him to write the introduction to his book. Fanon's relationship with Sartre always was ambivalent. As far as his theory was concerned, he owed him a great deal; not only do his early writings clearly show Sartre's influence but even certain aspects of his theory of violence are identical with ideas which

[1] Fanon obstinately refused to husband his energies as long as his activity was necessary for the revolution, even though the leaders of the GPRA had urged him to take care of himself in view of his illness. In her memoirs, Simone de Beauvoir describes Sartre's meeting with Fanon in Rome in August 1961, six months before the latter's death: 'We met Sartre for lunch. The conversation went on till two o'clock in the morning. I finally broke it off as politely as possible by explaining that Sartre needed some sleep. Fanon was outraged. "I don't like people who are chary of their energies", he said to Lanzmann, whom he forced to sit up with him till 8.00 a.m. Like the Cubans, the Algerian revolutionaries never slept more than four hours a night.' Simone de Beauvoir, *La Force des Choses* (Paris: Gallimard 1963), p. 619.

Sartre had developed in his *Critique de la Raison dialectique*. But at the same time he also saw him as the typical French intellectual that he himself was, or at least had been, and with whom he no longer wished, and was unable, to identify, without, however, giving up his own intellectuality. Simone de Beauvoir writes in her memoirs:

> Still, Fanon never forgot that Sartre was French, and he reproached him with not atoning for it sufficiently, "We have claims on you. How can you continue leading a normal life, and writing?" Now he requested of him to think of some efficacious line of action, now he wanted him to embrace the role of the martyr. He lived in a different world from our own. He was convinced that Sartre would rouse public opinion by declaring that he was going to give up writing until the end of the war. Alternatively, he should get himself imprisoned. That would cause a national scandal. We were unable to change his mind on this point.[1]

In autumn Fanon's health deteriorated even further. He travelled to Washington where he remained without any medical care for one week, due to administrative difficulties. When he was finally hospitalized, his state was beyond hope. While in hospital he received numerous visits from African UN representatives; he was still full of fighting spirit and outlined various projects of books he still wanted to write. At the end of November he received a copy of his book, *The Wretched of the Earth*, from his French publisher, Maspero. He died on 6 December, 1961.

Before his departure for the United States Fanon had expressed the wish to be taken back to Africa and to be buried in Algerian soil. His body was flown to Tunis by special plane and laid out in state at the seat of the GPRA. Krim Belkacem made a funeral oration. Then the coffin was taken to Gardimaou and handed over to the ALN who conveyed it through the battle

---

[1] de Beauvoir, La Force p. 624.

zone to Algerian territory. The commander of the 'Frontier Force', Colonel Boumedienne, gave a short commemorative address before Fanon was buried alongside other militants.

Four weeks prior to his death Fanon wrote to a friend, Roger Tayeb:

> Roger, what I wanted to tell you is that death is always with us and that what matters is not to know whether we can escape it but whether we have achieved the maximum for the ideas we have made our own. What shocked me here in my bed when I felt my strength ebbing away along with my blood was not the fact of dying as such, but to die of leukemia, in Washington, when three months ago I could have died facing the enemy since I was already aware that I had this disease. We are nothing on earth if we are not in the first place the slaves of a cause, the cause of the peoples, the cause of justice and liberty. I want you to know that even when the doctors had given me up, in the gathering dusk I was still thinking of the Algerian people, of the peoples of the Third World, and when I have persevered, it was for their sake.

Preface

THIS work proposes to present and analyse Frantz Fanon's theories. The category of alienation is a suitable means of discussing Fanon's analyses, which mostly relate to the growth of consciousness. The results of his investigations are of fundamental importance for the explanation of colonial and neocolonial phenomena. His approach to such problems shows that certain psychological and socio-psychological aspects of colonialism can only be adequately explained if historical, economic and psychodynamic criteria are an integral part of the analysis. On the other hand his publications bring home the fact that the political process of decolonization can be adequately interpreted only if the processes of consciousness and the psychological mechanisms produced by colonialism are taken into account. Any research into colonial phenomena runs the risk of getting bogged down in colonial, racialist or paternalistic categories if the psychological processes of oppression discussed by Fanon are neglected or passed over in silence. His theories are, however, limited in scope by the fact of their being based on the historico-economic and political conditions he encountered in his own revolutionary activity. His description of processes of alienation can in the first instance only claim validity for those areas which he knew from first-hand experience. To what extent his findings are of general applicability to all countries of the Third World remains to be further investigated.

Fanon's political experiences with both colonialism and the anticolonial liberation struggle are almost entirely restricted to Algeria. His analyses of racism are primarily derived from his experiences in the Caribbean and in France. If in this study we henceforth speak of colonialism, we therefore mean in the first place French colonialism. It is not, however, intended to pass a value judgment on the relative merits or demerits of the British and French colonial system such as can often be found in literature.[1] It is pointless to try and decide which of the systems was a trifle less inhuman, or whether French racism was less racist than, say, the British variety: 'A given society is racist or it is not. Unless this self-evident truth is understood, a great number of problems will be neglected'.[2]

As regards the aspects of colonialism which form the subject of this study, viz the forms of alienation brought about by the colonial situation, it is imperious that we should limit ourselves to the French colonies since the manifestations of cultural and psychological alienation presumably take various shapes, depending on whether a colonial policy is determined by the principle of 'indirect rule' and its latent apartheid tendencies, as in the British system, or by assimilation, as in the French system. There can be no doubt that by the very fact of idealizing assimilation, while at the same time brutally preventing its realization, the officially proclaimed assimilation policy of French colonialism contributed in no small measure to the specific phenomena of alienation and frustration analysed below.

---

1 See, e.g., George Padmore, *Panafricanism or Communism? The coming struggle for Africa* (New York: Roy Publishers, 1956), who by comparison considers the British colonial system the best. For the opposite view cf., e.g., A. Meister, *L'Afrique peut-elle partir?* (Paris: Editions du Seuil, 1966), pp. 89–90, who tries to prove that it was French assimilation policy in particular which was best at preparing the colonies for independence. (Author's note).
In the English translation of Meister's book, *East Africa: The Past in Chains, the Future in Pawn* (New York: Walker & Co., 1968), pp. 35–36, which is substantially abridged, the critical references to British colonialism are omitted. All quotations in the following are therefore translated from the French original. (Translator's note.)

2 Fanon, *Peau noire, masques blancs* (Paris: Editions du Seuil, 1952), p. 89.

1. Colonialism and Alienation

To begin with it has to be clarified whether the concept of alienation as evolved by Marx can be applied to the colonial situation, and whether the colonies, or the countries of the Third World in general, can be aptly analysed with reference to the economic categories Marx derived from capitalist commodity production, or whether the criteria of pre-capitalist conditions of production are not actually more suitable.

According to Marx pre-capitalist forms of production are characterized by the fact that the individuals as members of a community own the means of production, primarily the land. Under pre-capitalist conditions of production mainly articles of utility are produced, and payments in kind outweigh payments in money:

> In both forms (the small individual freehold as well as the communal type of land-ownership) the worker relates to the objective conditions of his labour as a property-owner; this is the natural unity of labour and its material prerequisites. The worker thus has an objective existence independent of his labour... In both forms the individuals do not behave as workers but as owners; they are members of a community and work as such.[1]

The conditions of labour being natural ones, they do not themselves appear as products of the working process; ownership of the land is a pre-condition of its being cultivated. The 'more or less historically developed

---

[1] Karl Marx, *Grundrisse der politischen Ökonomie* (Berlin: Rohentwurf, 1953), p. 375. See the chapter "Formen, die der kapitalistischen Produktion vorhergehen" pp. 375–413.

existence of the individual as member of a community, his natural existence (*naturwüchsiges Dasein*) as member of a tribe'[1] determines the relations of man to the land. 'In all forms where ownership of the land prevails, natural relationships are still predominant; in those where capital reigns, the social element created by history rules supreme.'[2] In these pre-bourgeois forms of society, where the separation of the producer from his means of production, the social division of labour and the production of commodities have not yet taken place, alienation in the sense Marx defined it, as deriving from the form of labour specific to bourgeois society, does not exist either.[3]

It is only under capitalist conditions of production, which are characterized by the separation of the producer from the means of production, that the object which labour produces—its product—is encountered as an alien entity, since it has taken the form of a commodity. The process through which the product, which is the objectification and realization of labour, becomes a commodity, changes its character: 'In the sphere of political economy this realization of labour appears as *loss of realization* for the workers, objectification as *loss of the object* and *bondage to it;* appropriation as *estrangement*, as *alienation*.'[4] The pivotal concept used by Marx to explain reification and alienation is alienated

---

[1] ibid., p. 385.

[2] Karl Marx, *Zur Kritik der politischen Ökonomie* (Berlin: Dietz, 1951), pp. 264–265.

[3] Karl Marx, *Ökonomisch-Philosophische Manuskripte (1844)*, in; K. Marx und F. Engels, *Werke*, Ergänzungsband, erster Teil (Berlin: 1968), pp. 530–531. 'Under the pretext of the recognition of man, national economy, whose principle is labour, on the contrary consistently practices the denial of man, for he no longer remains in a state of external tension with regard to the external essence of private property, but has himself become this essence of private property which is at conflict with itself. That which formerly was a being made external to itself, or a real externalization of man, now actually has become the act of externalization or of alienation."

[4] Karl Marx, *Economic and Philosophic Manuscripts of 1844* ed. D. J. Struik, (London: Lawrence and Wishart, 1970), p. 108. (Original italics

labour, which he deduced from the category of objectivization developed by Hegel in *The Phenomenology of Mind.* In the labour process man relates to himself and to his object; he is not identical with his labour but is capable of confronting and opposing the product of his own activity:

> The fact that man exists objectively "for himself" in the process of labour is intimately connected with the second fact that man is himself an "objective", or more precisely, an "objectifying" being. Man can only realize his essential nature by realizing it objectively, i.e., by producing, through the "forces of his being", an "external", "material", objective world, in the shaping of which through labour (in the widest acceptance of the word) he becomes his real self.[1]

Work is thus the human quality which, over and above the economic sphere, defines the essence of man. However, Marx criticizes Hegel for positing that consciousness objectifying itself should in this externalization remain in itself, that consequently alienation is cancelled and superseded only in appearance since the forms of estranged humanity specified by Hegel are not conceived of as forms of consciousness: 'Because in this manner only "conceived" but not "actual" forms of alienation are superseded, and because in consequence "this supersession through thought... leaves its object untouched in reality", Marx can say that the entire "phenomenology", or better still, the whole of the Hegelian system in so far as it is based on this "phenomenology", remains within the confines of alienation'.[2] According to Hegel the human being, which he conceives as knowledge, has to abandon itself to the object in order to realize itself; only in 'being other' can it achieve its own proper self-existence (*Fürsichsein*). Marx, on the other hand, no longer

---

[1] Herbert Marcuse, 'Neue Quellen zur Grundlegung des historischen Materialismus,' *Die Gesellschaft*, 9th year, no. 8, Berlin (1932), p. 145.

[2] ibid., p. 170.

conceives of objectifying labour merely as a stage in the process of the formation of consciousness but by approaching it from the materialist viewpoint sees it as social labour, as 'metabolism between man and nature'. He thus arrives at a concept of alienation which interprets the process of objectification as the reification of man in the capitalist society based on commodity exchange.

Marx exemplifies the alienation of labour in the relation of the producer to the product of his labour as well as in the relation of the worker to his own activity. In capitalist society the workers produce commodities, the production of which requires capital. The commodities are placed on the market by private entrepreneurs and sold with a view to increasing their capital through profits and enhancing further production of commodities. The worker, through his wage contract, surrenders to the capitalist the product of his labour which, having become a commodity, is subsequently made available to him on the market as an exchange value: 'The worker alienated from his product is at the same time alienated from himself. His labour itself becomes no longer his own, and the fact that it becomes the property of another bespeaks an expropriation that touches the very essence of man'.[1] In his early writings Marx conceives of alienation as reification (*Verdinglichung*), through which capitalist society causes all interpersonal relations to take the form of objective relations between things: 'Relations such as those between capital and labour, capital and commodity, and those between commodities are understood as human relations, relations in man's social existence ... The system of capitalism relates men to each other through the commodities which they

[1] Herbert Marcuse, *Reason and Revolution* (London: Routledge and Kegan Paul, 2nd ed., 1955), p. 277.

exchange'.[1] Man is alienated from himself, since under capitalist conditions of production he is incapable of objectifying himself through labour: 'Alienation manifests itself both through the fact that my means of subsistence belongs to another, that the object of my desire is the inaccessible property of another, and through the fact that each object as well as my own activity is alien to itself, since everything and everybody, the capitalist not excluded, is dominated by an inhuman power'.[2]

In his *Capital* Marx expounds the process of alienation as 'the fetishism of commodities', for the product of labour assumes the character of a commodity under the capitalist mode of production: 'To (the producers who make an exchange), their own social action takes the form of the action of objects, which rule the producers instead of being ruled by them'.[3] But he does not fail to observe that history, however 'natural', is also made by men, even though they might act without any conscious purpose or common will. The historical conditions which confront men always structure their actions: 'Men make their own history, but they do not make it just as they please; they do not make it under circumstances chosen by themselves, but under circumstances directly encountered, given and transmitted from the past'.[4] Only the abolition of capitalist class society by the socialist revolution will bring about the end of alienation. But in order to be able to make a revolution, the working class from being a class 'in itself' must become a class 'for itself', aware of its own

---

1 ibid, p. 278-279

2 Karl Marx, 'Nationalökonomie and Philosophie' (1844), in *Die Frühschriften* (Stuttgart: A. Kröner, 1953), p. 266.

3 Karl Marx *Capital* Vol. 1 (Moscow: Foreign Languages Publishing House, 1961), p. 75.

4 Karl Marx, 'The Eighteenth Brumaire of Louis Bonaparte', in Marx and Engels, *Selected Works in Two Volumes* Vol. 1 (Moscow: Foreign Languages Publishing House, 1951), p. 225.

proper self-existence; it must develop a class-consciousness. Each one of its members must be conscious of his alienation and its underlying economic causes. It is only such an insight into the mediation of the capitalist production process and one's own exploited and alienated existence that is capable of engendering a revolutionary class-consciousness and thus, in the long run, of superseding man's alienation.

Is the notion of alienation evolved by Marx and Hegel adequate for an analysis of colonial conditions? In order to answer this question, we must first determine the level of economic development of the so-called underdeveloped countries, that is to say all those countries which used to be, or still are, under colonial domination. Only very few of the countries now poor were not colonized. Bettelheim points out that these countries, although they may be referred to as backward do not, however, show the characteristics of underdevelopment—especially the criterion of integration into the world market.[1] The characteristic features of pre-capitalist modes of production as listed by Marx, especially the producers' ownership of the means of production and their integration in a corporate community, do not apply, or rather do not apply any longer, to the colonial economies. The intervention into the internal conditions of the colonies by the capitalist countries has modified their social and economic structures in such a way that a whole system of relationships between countries bent on capitalist expansion on the one hand, and their colonial dependencies on the other hand, has developed:

> Thus capitalist accumulation as a whole, as an actual historical process, has two different aspects. One concerns the commodity market and the place where surplus value is produced—the factory, the mine, the agricultural estate.

---

[1] See Charles Bettelheim, *Planification et croissance accélérée* (Paris: FM/Petite Collection Maspero, 1967), p. 29.

Regarded in this light, accumulation is a purely economic process, with its most important phase a transaction between the capitalist and wage labourer. In both its phases, however, it is confined to the exchange of equivalents and remains within the limits of commodity exchange. Here, in form at any rate, peace, property and equality prevail, and the keen dialectics of scientific analysis were required to reveal how the right of ownership changes in the course of accumulation into appropriation of other people's property, how commodity exchange turns into exploitation and equality becomes class-rule.

The other aspect of the accumulation of capital concerns the relations between capitalism and the non-capitalist modes of production which start making their appearance on the international stage. Its predominant methods are colonial policy, an international loan system—a policy of spheres of interest—and war.[1]

In the areas which had been forced to become the suppliers of raw materials for the metropolitan countries, colonialism reduced the natives to the status of proletarians who had to work in mines and on plantations. It would, however, hardly be correct to consider this process as a transition to a wage-labour relationship since in most cases it was actually a forced labour relationship, and payment was frequently made in kind. Even regions with feudal or semi-feudal forms of political organisation, which were only of secondary interest to the colonial power, succumbed to its indirect influence because the feudal structures were deformed by their isolation and by colonial measures such as taxation. The result was a stagnation of economic development in those areas. In any case, however, the intervention of the colonial power brought about the disruption of traditional structures and caused the dependent countries to dovetail into the system of exploitation through foreign capital.

---

[1] Rosa Luxemburg, *The Accumulation of Capital* (London: Routledge and Kegan Paul, 1951), p. 452.

> While the setting up of industries in the colonized countries served to destroy the existing pre-capitalist social structures and modes of production, the industrial impulses released by foreign investments tended to be fed back in the main to the Western societies. The deformed traditional systems were not superseded by a "higher", capitalist form of economic organization, but they became the organized hinterland of exploitation through foreign investments geared to the requirements of the capitalist societies themselves.[1]

Bettelheim defines the special economic characteristics of underdevelopment in negative terms in order to prove that colonialism has provoked structural changes which do not permit us to apply to this system the yardsticks elaborated for a pre-bourgeois European society:

> These countries, industrialized today, were not economically dependent. Their production was not structured in such a way that it had to accommodate hypertrophied sectors closely linked to overseas markets and strongly penetrated by foreign capital. These economies neither developed nor stagnated in consonance with the upward or downward trends of one raw material or another, of some primary agricultural product on the world market. They were not subject to heavy external commitments (interests, dividends, or royalties payable to foreign capitalists), and their nascent industry did not have to compete with powerful, well-established industries dominated by the same big capital which controlled their own natural resources... Even though these economies might show a low level of industrialization, they were not deformed or unbalanced but on the contrary integrated and centred upon themselves.[2]

It now remains for us to investigate the problem of to what extent colonial societies bear the imprint of the capitalist economic system. This question cannot be answered unequivocally and in such a way as to

---

[1] Conrad Schuhler, *Zur politischen Ökonomie der armen Welt* (Munich: Tricont, 1968), p. 100.

[2] Bettelheim, *Planification*, pp. 28–29.

apply equally to all colonial territories. Baran speaks of peoples in the Third World as finding themselves 'in the twilight of feudalism and capitalism':[1]

> By breaking up the age-old patterns of their agricultural economy, and by forcing shifts to the production of exportable crops, Western capitalism destroyed the self-sufficiency of their rural society that formed the basis of the pre-capitalist order in all countries of its penetration, and rapidly widened and deepened the scope of commodity circulation. By outright—in many countries, massive—seizure of peasant-occupied land for plantation purposes and other uses by foreign enterprise and by exposing their rural handicrafts to the withering competition of its industrial exports, it created a vast pool of pauperized labour. Enlarging thus the area of capitalist activities, it advanced the evolution of legal and property relations attuned to the needs of a market economy and established administrative institutions required for their enforcement.[2]

Andre Gunder Frank in his analysis of underdevelopment goes even a step further.[3] He explicitly refers to Baran's surplus theory,[4] which the latter developed in analysing the monopoly capitalist structure of the highly industrialized countries. Like Baran he starts from the premise that imperialism does not introduce industrial but rather mercantile capitalism in the underdeveloped countries. The wasting of potential

---

[1] Paul A. Baran, *Political Economy of Growth* (New York: Monthly Review Press, 1957), p. 144. Cf. in this context Marx's observations on British colonialism in India: 'This decline of Indian towns celebrated for their fabrics was by no means the worst consequence. British steam and science uprooted, over the whole surface of Hindustan, the union between agricultural and manufacturing industry ... English interference ... dissolved these small semi-barbarian, semi-civilized communities, by blowing up their economical basis ...' Karl Marx, 'The British Rule in India', in Marx and Engels, *Selected Works* I, pp. 315–317. Cf. also, Karl Marx, 'The Future Results of British Rule in India,' in *Selected Works* I, pp. 319–324, and Karl Marx, 'The Modern Theory of Colonization', *Capital, 1*, pp. 765–774.

[2] Baran, *Growth*, p. 143.

[3] See Andre Gunder Frank, *Capitalism and Underdevelopment in Latin America* (New York: Monthly Review Press, 1967).

[4] In determining economic surplus Baran distinguishes between *actual* economic surplus and *potential* economic surplus. The former is the difference between society's *actual* current output and its effective current consumption; it is

[*Notes continued on the next page*]

surplus, which in the underdeveloped satellites takes the form of unemployment, underemployment, inadequate utilization of the soil, and over/underproduction,[1] is here even more conspicuous than in the highly developed metropolitan countries. But even the actual surplus does not benefit the underdeveloped countries since it is mainly transferred to the metropolitan countries. 'My thesis is that these capitalist contradictions and the historical development of the capitalist system have generated underdevelopment in the peripheral satellites whose economic surplus was expropriated, while generating economic development in the metropolitan centres which appropriate that surplus—and, further, that this process still continues'.[2]

The world-wide process of capitalist development leads to a polarization between, on the one hand, highly developed, industrialized metropolitan countries and, on the other, stagnating satellites. 'From the very beginning the opening up of the dependent territories through capitalism took on a monopolistic complexion

---

generated in all economies, and its magnitude is, at least conceptually, readily established. *Potential* economic surplus is the difference between the output that *could* be produced under given circumstances with the help of employable productive resources, and what might be regarded as essential consumption. Its realization requires far-reaching changes in the structure of society. It appears under four headings: excess consumption on the part of certain classes of society; output lost to society through the existence of unproductive workers; output lost because of the wasteful organization of the existing productive apparatus; output foregone owing to the existence of unemployment and the deficiency of effective demand. 'The category of the potential economic surplus itself transcends the horizon of the existing social order, relating as it does not merely to the easily observable performance of the given socioeconomic organization, but also to the less readily visualized image of a more rationally ordered society'. Baran, *Growth*, p. 24. Also see Paul A. Baran and Paul M. Sweezy, *Monopoly Capital* (New York: Monthly Review Press, 1966).

1 Over/underproduction is a term used to describe a situation found in underdeveloped agrarian economies, in which the necessary means of subsistence are produced in such small quantities that they partly have to be imported and paid for in rare foreign exchange. Part of the population are on a starvation diet while at the same time export crops are produced in large quantities for the world market where more often than not they are sold at give-away prices.

2 Frank, *Capitalism and Underdevelopment*, p. 3.

and thus prevented the process of "division of labour through division of labour". No "normal" capitalist development could take place in the colonies, and not even the positive features of a capitalism based on market competition could ever be taken advantage of for supplying the domestic market.'[1] The metropolitan countries expropriate economic surplus from their satellites and appropriate it for their own development, while the latter stagnate in their underdevelopment, first because they lack access to their own surplus, and second because they have to bear the brunt of the metropolis/satellite polarization and the exploitative contradictions which the close ties with their respective metropolitan centres have introduced and perpetuated in the satellites' domestic economic structures.

Bourgeois as well as Marxist theoreticians have described this process, which is particularly advanced in South America, as 'dual economic development', a concept based on the assumption that there is a parallel development of capitalist and feudal economic structures. The thesis of dual economic development implies a linear progression from feudalism to capitalism similar to the European development of the last few centuries; the rural areas are still supposed to be feudal, while the urban ones are said to be already involved in the capitalist development process. Frank strongly objects to this thesis and tries to prove that in view of the international conditions of dependence existing within the framework of a polarized capitalist process one cannot justifiably speak of any feudal structure since even the supposedly feudal property structure in the country is subjected to decisions taken by the metropolitan countries. Even the most remote 'traditional' sectors of society, which one tends to refer to as feudal, are integrated into the capitalist system. Frank concludes

[1] Schuhler, *Politische Ökonomie der armen Welt*, p. 126

that under these circumstances it would be illusory to aspire to a modern capitalist development independent from imperialism. It would be equally wrong to expect the national bourgeoisie to change existing conditions. The reason why these phenomena have so frequently been misinterpreted is total ignorance of the fact that the historical process of capitalist expansion and development entails both economic development and, simultaneously, structural underdevelopment. Capitalism has always and everywhere produced this dual result. The error consists in defining capitalism according to metropolitan yardsticks. Frank summarizes the main characteristics of the metropolis/satellite model as follows: (*a*) close economic, political, social and cultural ties; total integration even of the most peripheral areas into the system; (*b*) monopolistic structure of the entire system; (*c*) misconceived planning and use of resources in all segments of the metropolis/satellite chain; and (*d*) as part of the misconceived use of resources, the expropriation and appropriation of the satellites' surplus by the local, regional, national and international metropolitan centres.

As an integral part of the capitalist system, the colonial economy is characterized by the separation of the majority of workers from the means of production, the abolition of older forms of ownership, and to a limited extent the division of labour, and wage-labour relationships. These criteria apply primarily to plantation and mining economies; as a general rule it can be said that the colonized people were compelled to gear their production to the demands of a market-economy, i.e., to cultivate products which they were no longer able to use for their own subsistence. However, one essential element of industrial capitalism which is of special importance with reference to phenomena of alienation is lacking in colonialism; there is neither a developed commodity production nor a developed commodity exchange which integrates people into society. The exchange does not take place on a market within the colonial society but it develops via the world-market between two societies, the metropolitan and the colonial one: 'Whatever market for manufactured goods emerged in the colonial and dependent countries did not become the "internal market" of these countries. Thrown wide open by colonization and by unequal treaties, it became an appendage of the "internal market" of Western capitalism'.[1] On the world market the form of the commodity conceals the dependence of the colony on the metropolis. The alienation brought about by colonialism is thus a double one. While in capitalism the exploitation takes place in the realm of production and while the exchange keeps at least a semblance of equivalence, the colonized is exploited twofold: first in his conditions of production by the colonial overlord, and secondly in his exchange relations by the metropolis.[2]

Since economic exchange relations as an element of integration are lacking, the racial ideology assumes a special function and becomes in fact an indispensable instrument in ensuring the cohesion of the colonial system, which is based on violence. The superiority of the colonizers, manifesting itself through brute force and legitimized in their own view by the alleged racial inferiority of the natives, is acknowledged by the oppressed themselves through the process of alienation. French assimilation policy is a case in point. Although it claimed to be non-racial in its basic assumptions, it offered only relatively few people the opportunity of rising from the level of natives to the status of human

---

[1] Baran, *Growth*, p. 174. See also Armando Córdova and Héctor Silva Michelena 'Die wirtschaftliche Struktur der unterentwickelten Länder', in *Die wirtschaftliche Struktur Lateinamerikas. Drei Studien zur politischen Ökonomie der Unterentwicklung* (Frankfurt a. M.: Suhrkamp, 1969).

[2] This economic derivation is hardly touched upon by Fanon. His concept of alientation—the alienation of man from his own potentialities—is close to Marx's analysis in his *Early Texts*.

beings through a process of Europeanization, i.e., complete alienation from their own history and culture. It thus caused frustrations, compensatory phenomena and cases of psycho-somatic illness, all of which have to be viewed as a result of colonial alienation.

As the absolute inability of the individual to recognize and develop himself and his own potentialities, alienation always has both economic and intellectual aspects. Fanon's interest is mainly focussed on an analysis of intellectual alienation (*aliénation intellectuelle*). All colonized people are subjected to the economic conditions of alienation, which he considers the constitutive elements of psychological phenomena of alienation; however, certain types of intellectual alienation can also appear in various forms in most of the colonized. In those groups which are most strongly exposed to the colonial ideology, i.e., mainly the *evolués*, alienation appears in overt psychic conflicts:

> In the first case (that of the intellectual), the alienation is of an almost intellectual character. In so far as he conceives of European culture as a means of stripping himself of his race, he becomes alienated. In the second case (that of the worker), it is a question of a victim of a system based on the exploitation of a given race by another, of the contempt in which a given branch of humanity is held by a form of civilization that pretends to superiority.[1]

Fanon's psychological-therapeutic approach,[2] which justifies an analysis of his entire work under the aspect of alienation, has a political objective; the 'intellectual alienation' of the colonized, which shows itself in their

---

1 Frantz Fanon, *Black Skin White Masks*, trans. C. L. Markmann (London: MacGibbon & Kee, 1968), p. 223.

2 Gerhard Grohs has characterized Fanon's method as follows: 'The relationships between white and black in a colonial society under the aspect of alienation are the subject of this book (*Black Skin*). The author approaches it with a method which he himself terms psychoanalytical but which in actual fact is a synthesis of sociological, psychological and Marxian concepts'. Gerhard Grohs, 'Frantz Fanon, ein Theoretiker der afrikanischen Revolution', *Kölner Zeitschrift für Soziologie und Sozialpsychologie* 16. Jhrg., Heft 3, Cologne and Opladen (1964): 458.

identification with a racial stereotype and causes all kinds of frustrations and complexes, prevents the exploited from gaining an insight into their economic plight and gauging it in terms of their own position as a class. As long as their consciousness is structured by racialist norms they are incapable of developing a revolutionary class-consciousness.

It would, therefore, not be fully justified to criticize Fanon for neglecting economic factors. His analysis specifically deals with psychological phenomena which no investigation of colonialism and neocolonialism along economic lines can afford to overlook. Furthermore, the phenomena of alienation caused by racism objectively take on a special relevance in view of the absence of exchange relations in the colonies.

In a brief chapter of his book *Black Skin White Masks* entitled, 'The Negro and Hegel'[1] Fanon makes use of Hegel's analysis of the relationship between lord and bondsman to elucidate the problem which is at the centre of his own theoretical endeavour. As his point of departure he quotes Hegel's proposition, 'Self-consciousness exists in itself and for itself, in that, and by the fact that it exists for another self-consciousness; that is to say, it *is* only by being acknowledged or "recognized".[2] At the foundation of the dialectic of lordship and bondage there is an absolute reciprocity, which is the precondition of liberation:

> The process then is absolutely the double process of both self-consciousnesses. Each sees the other do the same as itself; each itself does what it demands on the part of the other, and for that reason does what it does, only so far as the other does the same. Action from one side would be useless, because what is to happen can only be brought about by means of both . . . They recognize themselves as mutually recognizing one another.[3]

---

[1] Fanon, *Black Skin*, pp. 216–222.

[2] G. W. F. Hegel, *The Phenomenology of Mind*, rev. 2nd ed. (London: Allen & Unwin, 1949), p. 229.

[3] Hegel, *Phenomenology of Mind*, pp. 230–231.

The element of recognition is lacking in the relationship between the white master and the black bondsman. The white man accepted the Negro when he abolished slavery, but no true emancipation has taken place since the Negro did not emancipate himself: 'Historically, the Negro steeped in the inessentiality of servitude was set free by his master. He did not fight for his freedom'.[1] The transformation reached the Negro from without; instead of acting, he was acted upon, his change of status from slave to bondsman remained external to him: 'The Negro is a slave who has been allowed to assume the attitude of a master. The white man is a master who has allowed his slaves to eat at his table'.[2] But as long as the Negro has not endeavoured to free himself, he will continue imitating his white master; as long as his fixation to the white man exists, he cannot turn freely towards the world. The difference between the bondsman/master relationship in Hegel, and the black/white relationship is of fundamental importance: 'In Hegel the slave turns away from the master and turns towards the object. Here the slave turns toward the master and abandons the object'[3]

What is decisive for the absence of reciprocal recognition between the white man and the Negro is the fact that no struggle has taken place between them. Fanon quotes Hegel: 'The relation of both self-consciousnesses is in this way so constituted that they prove themselves and each other through a life-and-death struggle . . . The individual, who has not staked his life, may, no doubt, be recognized as a *person*, but he has not attained the truth of this recognition as an independent self-consciousness'.[4] While the American Negroes are already engaged in fighting for their

---

[1] Fanon, *Black Skin*, p. 219.
[2] ibid., p. 219.
[3] ibid., p. 221, fn. 8.
[4] Hegel, *Phenomenology of Mind*, pp. 232–233.

freedom, the Africans, oppressed by colonialism, have not yet seized this opportunity: 'But the Negro knows nothing of the cost of freedom, for he has not fought for it'.[1] The question is, however, whether the same does not likewise apply to European conditions and whether Hegel's dialectical turn is not only an idealistic one. Neither did the bourgeoisie in its struggle for emancipation succeed in freeing itself entirely from feudal structures—in Germany, if not in other countries, its basic aspirations for self-realization were not so much aimed at constituting a class of its own as at being admitted to the social sphere of the nobility—nor did the proletariat succeed in its emancipation as the working class. There was no revolution. This digression may have helped to throw light on the question why Fanon attached such great importance to detecting the mechanisms of alienation, and which were the *praxis*-oriented political intentions informing the theory he elaborated.[2]

---

[1] Fanon, *Black Skin*, p. 221.

[2] For a more detailed discussion of Fanon's reception of Hegel in the context of his theory of violence see chapters six and seven.

2. The Colonial Situation

A SHORT description of the colonial situation will throw into relief its special socio-psychological aspects which are characteristic of the phenomena analysed by Fanon. The term 'colonial situation' is used in a similar way by such authors as Memmi,[1] Sartre[2] or Balandier[3]; it stresses the reciprocal structural dependence of metropolis and colony and serves as a backdrop to a valid analysis of the interdependence of *colon* and *colonisé*. This overview is by no means in contrast to a specifically economic analysis, although it lays greater emphasis on the ideological implications and the socio-psychological consequences of the process of colonization.

The field of force of the colonial situation is marked by two antagonistic poles: the colonizer and the colonized. The prosperity and privileges of the former are directly based on the exploitation and pauperization of the other. In order to maintain this condition, the act of oppression must be constantly reproduced: 'For it is the settler who has brought the native into existence and who perpetuates his existence. The settler owes the fact of his very existence, that is to say his

---

[1] See Albert Memmi, *Portrait du colonisé précédé du portrait du colonisateur* (Paris: Pauvert, 1966).

[2] See Jean-Paul Sartre, 'Colonialisme et Néocolonialisme', in *Situations V* (Paris: N.R.F., Gallimard, 1964).

[3] See Georges Balandier, *The Sociology of Black Africa*, trans. Douglas Garman (London: André Deutsch, 1970). Part I, 'The 'Colonial Situation'' and its Negation, pp. 21–81.

property, to the colonial system'.[1] The most characteristic feature of the colonial situation is racism, which underpins ideologically the division of society into 'human beings' and 'natives' caused by the colonial process of production: 'For the one, privilege and humanity are one and the same thing; he makes himself into a man by freely excercising his rights. As for the other, the absence of any rights sanctions his misery, his chronic hunger, his ignorance, in short, his subhuman status'.[2] Racism endows the colonial system with cohesion. By reducing the native to a natural object, a chattel,[3] it enables the European to cleave to the ideals of Western democracy while at the same time exploiting the natives in the most inhuman fashion.

> Everyone has felt the contempt implicit in the term "native", used to designate the inhabitants of a colonized country. The banker, the manufacturer, even the professor in the home country, are not natives of any country: they are not natives at all. The oppressed person, on the other hand, feels himself to be a native; each single event in his life repeats to him that he has not the right to exist.[4]

However, the reactions of the indigenes themselves to racial discrimination have a stabilizing effect on the system. In the same measure as the oppressed learn to perceive the cause of their oppression in their own inferiority, their power of resistance weakens. Under the pressure of the prejudices mobilized against them they act against their own interests. Racial prejudice so

---

1 Frantz Fanon, *The Wretched of the Earth*, preface by Jean-Paul Sartre, trans. Constance Farrington (London: MacGibbon & Kee, 1965), p. 30.

2 Jean-Paul Sartre, preface to Memmi, *Portrait du Colonisè*, p. 34.

3 ibid. Also see Aimé Césaire, *Discours sur le colonialisme* (Paris: Présence Africaine, 1955), p. 22. Césaire here speaks of the equation 'colonisation—chosification' Also see François Perroux, *Coexistence*, 2 vols (Paris: P.U.F, 1958), p. 179 'The slave is not recognized by his obedience and by the hardness of his toil but by his reduction to an instrument and his transformation into a thing.'

4 J. P. Sartre, 'Materialism and Revolution', in *Literary and Philosophical Essays*, trans. A. Michelson (London: Hutchinson, 1968), p. 215.

glibly denies the native his quality of a 'human being' because the colonial system deprives him of all material means which would enable him to undergo the process of individuation. The oppressor thus produces and perpetuates the misery which in his view increasingly makes the oppressed the kind of creature that 'deserves such a fate'. 'Terror and exploitation dehumanize, and the exploiter uses this dehumanization as a pretext to step up his exploitation.'[1]

However, exploitation has its limit in the colonial system itself. The oppression must not lead to the negation of the colonized, to his physical annihilation, since such a state of affairs would also imply the negation of the colonizer: 'He must deny the colonized with all his strength, and at the same time the existence of his victim is indispensable to the continuance of his own being . . . *Were the colonized to disappear, the whole of colonization including the colonizer would disappear with him*'.[2] Memmi emphasizes the objective character of colonial conditions of production, which assign each one his social role under penalty of destruction. Thus there are neither good nor evil colonizers; their conduct is dictated to them by the function they occupy in the process of production. Even the newcomer from the metropolis soon grows aware of the reasons for his relative prosperity and does not fail to recognize the relation between his own privileged existence and the misery of the colonized. He finds himself as it were on the one scale of the balance, while the colonized are sitting on the other. The higher his standard of living, the lower is that of the colonized; the more deeply he breathes the more the other suffocates. Of course not all Europeans in the colonies are great landowners or high-ranking administrators; a majority of them are

---

[1] Sartre, preface to Memmi, *Portrait du Colonisé*, p. 36.
[2] Memmi, *Portrait du Colonisé*, pp. 92, 181.

themselves economically dependent upon the capitalist process of production. Nonetheless it is they who are more often than not the most fervent apologists of colonial privileges; they defend their superior economic status against the natives, however relative this superiority might be. In order to preserve their limited advantages, they have to identify with the very same economically powerful interests whose victims they themselves are. The sheer tenuousness of the economic basis on which their privileges repose makes them the fierce opponents they are of the colonial people.

In drawing his portrait of the colonizer Memmi distinguishes between the man of good intentions ('le colonisateur qui se refuse') and the die-hard colonialist ('le colonisateur qui s'accepte'). Given the specific situation of colonialism, the former's position soon turns out to be untenable as it implies the abolition of the colonial system. Any effective assimilation accompanied by the granting of equality to the natives would deprive colonial society of its very foundation. The well-intentioned colonist who tries to reject the colonialist ideology while at the same time maintaining its objective conditions is reduced to registering a merely abstract moral protest. The die-hard, on the other hand, by taking advantage of all the opportunities the system offers him and by cynically clamouring for even more privileges, shows greater consistency in his conduct; he defends his interests, availing himself of all means at his disposal to put through his claims. But even he is faced with the problem of legitimizing his privileges. This is achieved by the debasement of the colonized; by making him an untutored 'savage' in need of protection he justifies the colonizing function as that of a progressive pioneer, promoter and protector. In this rationalizing process the characteristic mediocrity of the colonizer, which is due to his stultifying social isolation on the one hand, and to his former social position in the metropolitan country on the other,[1] proves a veritable asset; it makes him equally susceptible to racism and to a sense of the white man's civilizing mission, which serve to conceal the bald economic facts. The Christian missions play an important role in this respect; by condemning the customs and religions of the natives as heathen and inhuman, they bolster and uphold colonial racism ideologically. At the same time they weaken the power of resistance of the indigenous population. Those converted to Christianity view their own culture and history as strange and become more receptive to colonial propaganda.

> . . . the triumphant *communiqués* from the missions are in fact a source of information concerning the implantation of foreign influences in the core of the colonized people . . . The Church in the colonies is the white people's Church, the foreigner's Church. She does not call the native to God's ways but to the ways of the white man, of the master, of the oppressor . . .[2]

The racial stereotype of the colonized designed by the colonizer is eventually adopted by the former. In social psychology this process, which in many cases even leads to self-hatred on the part of the victims of prejudice, is seen as one of many possible reactions of an out-group (the colonized people) to the prejudices of an in-group (their colonial overlords). Usually the out-group, which becomes the object of prejudices, is

---

[1] See the characterization of British settlers in Kenya in Meister, 'Les communautés des colons', p. 109. After the Second World War the new arrivals were almost entirely drawn from the ranks of war veterans.

[2] Fanon, *The Wretched*, p. 34. See also Wilhelm Reich, *Der Einbruch der Sexualmoral* (Berlin: Verlag für Sexualpolitik, 1932), p. 134. 'It does not take a great deal of education but only a little intellectual courage to recognize the fact that the capitalist powers do not bring the Christian faith, dress and "morality" to the colonial people out of a concern for civilization, but because these innovations are instrumental in inculcating in the individuals the spirit of the European coolies. Furthermore, they want to weaken them by alcohol and thus make them subservient. This inculcation of capitalism in the psychic structures of the primitives, which is to save overseers and police batons, is best accomplished by subjugating the revolutionary force born from a sated sexuality.'

a minority. In the case of colonialism, however, the repression is directed against the great majority of the population. It is practiced by a minority which is a minority only in terms of numbers but not in the sociological sense. 'There does not appear to have been adequate recognition of the paradoxical fact that the mentality of many Africans, in their own country, was in some ways characteristic of minority groups elsewhere.'[1] The adoption of the racial stereotype by the colonized themselves is a typical example of the self-fulfilling prophecy:[2] in view of the fact that the members of the out-group, surrendering to the constant pressure of discrimination, both institutional and personal, end up by actually developing the features ascribed to them by the racial stereotype, the members of the in-group see themselves confirmed in their prejudices. What began as a figment of the imagination eventually becomes a reality. This process is accelerated by the real sanctions and administrative measures which draw their justification from the racial fiction: the colonized is lazy, hence punitive measures are legitimate; he is unproductive, hence he has to be paid low wages; he is stupid, hence he must be protected in his own interest; he is savage and a slave to his instincts, hence police brutality and 'stern justice' are necessary to control him . . . The fact that many of the characteristics attributed to the native are mutually exclusive in no way alters the effectiveness of the clichés. They fulfill both economic and emotional functions for the colonizer. Excluded from all social institutions, cut off from his own history, deprived of his own language and of all possibilities of untrammelled self-expression, the colonized is left with only

---

[1] Gustav Jahoda, *White Man* (London: Oxford University Press, 1961), p. 115.
[2] See R. K. Merton, *Social Theory and Social Structure* (Glencoe: Free Press, 1957), p. 423: 'The self-fulfilling prophecy is, in the beginning, a *false* definition of the situation evoking a new behaviour which makes the originally false conception come *true*.'

two alternatives: open revolt or withdrawal to his own traditional institutions and values, such as the family and religion, which have however already been divested of their former vital functions by the contact with colonialism. Memmi speaks of an escape to the 'valeurs refuges', which he sees as a complementary phenomenon to the coercion applied from outside.

The process which transforms the immigrant from Europe into a colonialist also alienates him from his mother-country. As soon as the metropolis starts questioning the profitability of the established colonial system, the settlers try to maintain the traditional system of exploitation independently of the 'mother-country', as was the case, e.g., in Algeria and Rhodesia. The process of colonization, which initially was based on the purely economic motivations of the metropolis, thus develops its own inherent psychodynamic laws which may eventually lead to a complete break with the metropolis: 'Colonization produces the colonized just as we have seen it produce the colonizers'.[1] Crass exploitation is necessarily camouflaged by a smoke-screen of rationalizations and mystifications which in the long run affect both the colonizer and the colonized. The dehumanization of the oppressed falls back on the oppressor, thus finally leading to his own alienation. Colonial conquest, colonial administration and exploitation, acts which are based on the oppression of the natives, although they tend to be justified as attempts to bring them up to the level of rational human beings, have an inherent tendency to change the exploiter himself. In the same measure as the colonizer falls into the habit of seeing the colonized as a thing or treating him like an animal, he himself assumes inhuman features.

---

[1] Memmi, *Portrait du colonisé*, p. 128.

> When all is said and done the colonizer must be recognized by the colonized. The bond between colonizer and colonized is thus both destructive and creative. It destroys and recreates the two partners in the colonization process as colonizer and colonized: the former is disfigured into an oppresssor, an uncouth, fragmented human being, a cheat solely preoccupied with his privileges, the latter into a victim of oppression, broken in his development and accepting his own degradation.[1]

In his description of the colonial world Fanon places the emphasis on the violent character of this dualism: 'The dividing line, the frontiers are shown by barracks and police stations'.[2] In marked contrast to Europe, where capitalist norms have been interiorized in a long historical process, the colonies are a place where brute, immediate force rules supreme, where contact with the colonized is maintained by policemen and soldiers. This compartmentalized world is inhabited by two kinds of human beings: the natives and the 'others'. Like Memmi, Fanon points out the depersonalization discernible in the relations between *colon* and *colonisé*, which must be ascribed to racism. For the other, one only exists in the plural, any differentiation turns out to be impossible. Ezekiel Mphahlele, the exiled South African writer, declared in an interview: 'As to the whites, all I know about them is what one usually knows about people on the other side of the fence ... White people are mere outlines to me, they remain faceless. They're white, that's all'.[3] The colonial world is a Manichean world, in which 'the settler paints the native as a sort of

---

[1] ibid., p. 126. Jacques Berque writes in a similar vein, 'The colonizer, being influenced by the reaction of the colonized more than he thinks, increasingly attunes his own conduct to this reaction... Each of the two opponents thus remakes the other and destroys him in destroying himself'. Jacques Berque, a *Dépossession du monde* (Paris: Editions du Seuil, 1964), p. 95.

[2] Fanon, *The Wretched*, p. 31.

[3] Quoted from Meister, *L'Afrique peut-elle partir?*, p. 104.

quintessence of evil'.[1] What matters in the colony is not so much the individual's position in the process of production but rather his belonging to a race:

> In the colonies the economic substructure is also a superstructure. The cause is the consequence; you are rich because you are white, you are white because you are rich. This is why Marxist analysis should always be slightly stretched everytime we have to do with the colonial problem . . . It is neither the act of owning factories, nor estates, nor a bank balance which distinguishes the governing classes. The governing race is first and foremost those who come from elsewhere, those who are unlike the original inhabitants, "the others".[2]

While Memmi reveals the mechanisms, devised by the racialist ideology, which aim at camouflaging the hard facts of colonialism, Fanon in his main work, *The Wretched of the Earth*, emphasizes the significance of violence in the colonial system. This shift of emphasis is an expression of the different historical circumstances under which these two analyses were written. Memmi wrote his portrait of the colonizers and the colonized before the Algerian war, whereas Fanon developed his 'theory of violence' out of the *praxis* of the Algerian liberation struggle. In his first book, *Peau noire masques blancs*, he too had studied the racial foundations of colonialism in detail, approaching his subject from a psychological angle. We first want to discuss this phase of Fanon's thought, which was not yet explicitly concerned with the colonial situation as such but dealt specifically with white racism directed against the blacks. The title of his book, *Peau noire masques blancs* (*Black Skin*, *White Masks*) hints at his basic orientation, which is to investigate the process that makes coloured people into whites, thus creating a new species—the 'Greco-Latin Negroes'.[3]

---

1 Fanon, *The Wretched*, p. 33.
2 ibid., pp. 32–33.
3 This term was coined by Sartre in his preface to Fanon, *The Wretched*, p. 7.

3. The Function of Racism

IN undertaking his analysis, Fanon neither makes a scholarly contribution to the investigation of racial prejudice, nor does he take into account the findings of relevant researches in social psychology and psychoanalysis. His real intention would seem to be a formulation of his own experiences for practical purposes. He explicitly rejects a treatment of racism free from value judgments: 'I have not wished to be objective. Besides, that would be dishonest: It is not possible for me to be objective'.[1] At the same time he refuses to be identified with the attempt to establish the equality of races through an abstract approach. If it is necessary to bring in philosophy for this purpose, philosophy, according to Fanon, must be formalistic and inhuman: '. . . for, if philosophy and intelligence are invoked to proclaim the equality of men, they have also been employed to justify the extermination of men'.[2]

Fanon formulates his own experiences with the intention of demonstrating to his fellow-sufferers the socio-psychological mechanisms which conceal the causes of their oppression. As a medical doctor, and a black man in a white world, he wants to help them rid themselves of the complexes to which they have fallen

---

[1] Frantz Fanon, *Black Skin White Masks*, trans. C. L. Markmann (London: MacGibbon & Kee, 1968).

[2] ibid., p. 29 See T. W. Adorno, *Minima Moralia* (Frankfurt a. M.: Suhrkamp p. 11962),30: 'If on the other hand one were to postulate as an ideal the equality of all that bears a human face, instead of taking it for granted, this would not be of much avail. The abstract utopia might all too easily improve compatible with the most atrocious tendencies of society.'

victim owing to the impact of colonialism: 'This book, it is hoped, will be a mirror with a progressive infrastructure, in which it will be possible to discern the Negro on the road to disalienation'.[1] The black man must be made to realize that his alienation is not an individual problem. Its causes can be found in the interiorization of an historically and economically determined 'inferiority': 'If there is an inferiority complex, it is the outcome of a double process—primarily, economic—subsequently, the internalization, or, better, the epidermalization, of this inferiority'.[2]

Fanon starts from premises similar to those of Sartre in his essay on anti-Semitism, *Réflexions sur la question juive:* anti-Semitic prejudices are not derived from the historical existence of the Jews as such; what matters is the Jewish stereotype, which takes on an autonomous existence and serves as a scapegoat to camouflage and explain away the inherent antagonisms of capitalist class-society. It is only prejudice which makes the individual a 'Jew' in the anti-Semitic sense. There is no 'Jewish character' calling forth anti-Semitism, but 'the anti-Semite creates the Jew'.[3] Anti-Semitism conjures up the illusion of national unity without changing in the least the class character of society. Sartre comes to the conclusion that only a classless society will create the conditions capable of rendering anti-Semitism; and for that matter any other form of racism, redundant.

---

[1] Fanon, *Black Skin*, p. 184.

[2] ibid., p. 13.

[3] J. P. Sartre, *Réflexions sur la question juive* (Paris: Gallimard, 1954), p. 173. Cf. the findings in T. W. Adorno *et al., ed., The Authoritarian Personality* (New York: Harper, 1950), Part 4, p. 609: 'Here we limit ourselves to some extreme but concrete evidence of the fact that anti-Semitism is not so much dependent upon the nature of the object as upon the subject's own psychological wants and needs'.

Fanon's approach in analysing the mechanisms of racial discrimination and its ideological function in the process of colonial exploitation is similar to Sartre's. The person who has an excessive admiration for Negroes is as much of a racist as the one who despises them; the black man who wishes to bleach his race so as to become 'whiter and whiter every generation' is as miserable as the one who preaches hatred against the whites. The white society in which he lives constantly reminds the black man of his being different, either by friendly curiosity and overpoliteness or by outright discrimination. The white man's attitude towards blacks tends to show the features of adult behaviour towards children. He uses a simplified language with all the characteristics of infantile regression ('pidgin-nigger') irrespective of how good or bad a command of the white man's language the person thus addressed has. Often this type of discrimination is unintentional and casual, but it is the very matter-of-factness and indifference of such behaviour which most emphatically shows the Negro his place:

> "Look, a Negro!" The circle was drawing a bit tighter.
> "Mama, see the Negro! I'm frightened!"
> Frightened! Frightened!
> Now they were beginning to be afraid of me. I made up my mind to laugh myself to tears, but laughter had become impossible . . .
> "Look at the nigger! . . . Mama, a Negro!". . .
> "Hell, he's getting mad . . ."
> "Take no notice, sir, he does not know that you are as civilized as we . . ."
>
> My body was given back to me sprawled out, distorted, recoloured, clad in mourning in that white winter day. The Negro is an animal, the Negro is bad, the Negro is mean, the Negro is ugly; look, a nigger, it's cold, the nigger is shivering because he is cold, the little boy is trembling because he is afraid of the nigger, the nigger is shivering with cold . . . the handsome little bcy throws himself into his mother's arms: "Mama, the nigger's going to eat me up . . ."

> All this whiteness that burns me . . . I slip into corners . . . nigger underwear smells of nigger—nigger teeth are white—nigger feet are big—the nigger's barrel chest—I slip into corners, I remain silent, I strive for anonymity, for invisibility. Look, I will accept the lot, as long as no one notices me![1]

In the same measure as his inferiority is intimated to the Negro he suffers from not being white. His desire to be white is an indictment of the racialist structure of society, which is the true cause of his neurosis. Fanon reaches a conclusion similar to Sartre's: 'It is the racist who creates his inferior'.[2] He illustrates the racism of 'white' society directed against the blacks with a variety of examples drawn from literature, films and from his practice as a psychiatrist.[3] He points out that in Europe the 'black' stereotype has been associated with negative qualities (hell, devil, black soul, dirt, etc.) from time immemorial: 'In Europe whether concretely or symbolically, the black man stands for the bad side of the character'.[4] These stereotypes are imparted to children at a very tender age through fairy tales and educational maxims taking the form of proverbs: '. . . it would be impossible to ascribe too much importance to the way in which white children establish contact with the reality of the Negro'.[5] Like the Jew, the Negro is overdetermined (*sur-déterminé*) by his environment, but according to Fanon he is not only a slave to the idea others have of him but also a prisoner of his own body. While the Jew as a white man can integrate himself, at least temporarily, into a white society, the Negro can be identified everywhere and at any time by his outward appearance. Psychologically speaking he permanently

---

1 Fanon, *Black Skin*, pp. 111–116.
2 ibid., p. 93.
3 ibid., 'The Negro and Psychopathology' (chapter six) in particular, pp. 166–209.
4 ibid., p. 189.
5 ibid., p. 173.

finds himself, as it were, in the position of the Jew compelled to wear the yellow star.[1] This biological aspect is the palpable, inescapable element which the racialist ideology uses as its starting-point. In the web of race prejudice 'the Negro symbolizes the biological danger, the Jew, the intellectual danger'. To prove this thesis, Fanon quotes the findings of an investigation he carried out himself over several years. Out of 500 whites, about sixty percent associated the word 'Negro' with biology, sex, strong, athletic, potent, boxer, Joe Louis, Jesse Owens, Senegalese riflemen, savage, animal-like, devil, sin.[2] The bourgeois nostalgia for exoticism and its concomitant hatred for all those who are supposed to enjoy such freedom presumably constitutes a further element that plays an important role in anti-Negro prejudice:

> Traces of this behaviour pattern are still to be found in the attitudes of northern peoples toward southern ones. The well-to-do Puritans seek in vain in the dark-haired ladies of foreign lands what the course of the world ordained by them has taken away not only from themselves but even more from those that roam freely. The sedentary species envies the nomad and his search for green pastures . . . An infantile longing, moving aimlessly in circles, spending itself in an unhappy, restless urge to live and go on living, takes the place of undefiled fulfilment, which it precludes at the same time, because in its innermost self it resembles the self-preservation from which it pretends to free itself. Such is the circle of the bourgeois quest for naturalness.[3]

Among the multitude of clichés mobilised against the Negro the sexual aspect takes on a special significance: 'But it is in his corporeality that the Negro is

---

[1] Although Fanon here insists on the differences in psychological motivation with regard to anti-Semitism on the one hand and negrophobe racism on the other, on another occasion he stresses their relatedness: ethnocentric prejudice shows evidence of a high correlation between anti-Semitism and Negrophobia. See the relevant findings in Adorno *et al.*, *The Authoritarian Personality*, Part 1, chapter 4, 'The Study of Ethnocentric Ideology'.

[2] Fanon, *Black Skin*, pp. 165–166.

[3] Theodor W. Adorno, 'Prinzessin Eidechse, in *Minima Moralia*, pp. 223–224.

attacked. It is as a concrete personality that he is lynched. It is as an actual being that he is a threat.'[1] One attributes to the Negro an abnormal sexual potency bordering on the perverse. Fanon corroborates this thesis by his own experience as a practicing psychiatrist: in all cases of negrophobia the patients' sex life was found to be abnormal.[2] He assumes that the hatred of the whites against the Negroes stems from a feeling of sexual inferiority. Consequently, the lynching of a Negro would have to be interpreted as sexual revenge. Fanon implies that historically speaking intellectual progress entails a loss of sexual potential. Thus he interprets racism as the projection of the civilized white man's irrational longing for the lost paradise of sexual licence onto the Negro: 'Projecting his own desires onto the Negro, the white man behaves "as if" the Negro really had them'.[3] He fails to mention, however, that the historico-economic process of colonization which racism helps to rationalize demands of the ruling group that they renounce any display of spontaneity. Society imposes on its members a repressive regimentation of their instinctual economy.[4] Industrialization and an increasing socialization break in the individual for his role in the production process at the expense of his free sexual development. However, this type of repression is by no means a *sine qua non* of historical progress, although social evolution up to the present time has been increasingly characterized by processes of repressive interiorization. It is in fact inappropriate simply to identify historical processes with intellectual progress in general, and in this respect Fanon's analysis

---

[1] Fanon, *Black Skin*, p. 163.

[2] ibid., pp. 158–159. It should be noted, however, that the same phenomenon can be assumed in all extreme cases.

[3] ibid., p. 165.

[4] See Norbert Elias, *Über den Prozess der Zivilisation*, vol. 2 (Basel: Haus zum Falken, 1939), Summary 1, 'The social control of self-control', and 7, 'Greater cohesion of the upper class, stronger pressure from below'.

comes close to being itself an ideology. Furthermore, whether sexuality in its most consummate and orgiastic form can be more easily achieved in the state of nature than in civilization is a moot point: 'Strictly speaking, nature does not know enjoyment; it only realizes the gratification of wants. All pleasure is social, as much in its unsublimated passions as in its sublimated ones. It derives from alienation'.[1] Without expressly referring to it, Fanon bases his interpretation on Freud's theory which defines instinctual sublimation as one of the techniques of fending off suffering. Freud compares the satisfaction derived, e.g., from a sublimated artistic activity to the gratification of wild instinctual impulses and characterizes it as follows: 'At present we can only say figuratively that such satisfactions seem "finer and higher". But their intensity is mild compared with that derived from crude and primary instinctual impulses; it does not convulse our physical being'.[2] But the major objection to this is that a work of art can certainly not have as its basis the psychic deformation of the artist. Adorno terms Freud's theory of sublimation a 'psychoanalytical illusion': 'Art is as averse to art as is the artist. While ostensibly renouncing the object of its libido it nevertheless remains faithful to it, thus unmasking the socially desirable element which Freud naively glorifies as sublimation but which is probably non-existent'.[3] It is, therefore, doubtful whether Freud's theory of sublimation can be adopted unquestioningly, as is done by Fanon.

---

1 Max Horkheimer and Theodor W. Adorno, *Dialektik der Aufklärung* (Amsterdam: Querido, 1947), p. 127.

2 Sigmund Freud, *Civilization and its Discontents* (London: The Hogarth Press, 1963), pp. 16–17. See also the following quotation: 'Here, as we already know, civilization is obeying the laws of economic necessity, since a large amount of the psychical energy which it uses for its own purposes has to be withdrawn from sexuality'. Ibid., p. 41.

3 Adorno, *Minima Moralia,* pp. 284–286 ('Exhibitionist'). Wilhelm Reich writes: 'Sexual satisfaction is not opposed to the sublimation of sexual urges

[*Notes continued on the next page*]

In marked contrast to Sartre's analysis, which ultimately interprets racism as the ideology of a class-society, Fanon here still confines himself to a psychological approach. He does not view social inhibitions, which on the one hand rouse in man the longing for a liberated sexuality, while on the other prompt him to react jealously and viciously to any symptoms of such oftentimes imaginary freedom, within the context of capitalist conditions of production but interprets them abstractly as the result of intellectual progress. But elsewhere he goes a step further by insisting that the problem cannot be restricted to black people living among whites but has to be analyzed in conjunction with the whole of capitalist society. This contradiction between abstract formulations referring to economic conditions, and a concrete analysis dominated by psychology and thus disregarding its own premise, is typical of Fanon's early writings. In the same measure, however, as the focus of his research changes from the phenomenon of the 'metropolis' to the conditions in the colonies, economic aspects gain in importnce. Looking critically at his first book, he writes in an article published in 1955: 'Here we have proof that questions of race are but a superstructure, a mantle, an obscure ideological emanation concealing an economic reality'.[1]

---

in the working process; on the contrary, a good working performance presupposes the former. The relation between sexual satisfaction and sublimation is not a mechanical ('the more sexual repression the higher the social output') but a dialectical one. Sexual energy can be sublimated to a certain extent; if the deflection becomes excessive, the boosting effect of sublimation abruptly changes into its opposite, viz. a hampering of the capacity to work'. W. Reich, *Der Einbruch der Sexualmoral* (Berlin: Verlag für Sexualpolitik, 1932), pp. 129–130.

[1] F. Fanon, 'West Indians and Africans', in *Toward the African Revolution*, trans. Haakon Chevalier (New York: Monthly Review Press, 1967), p. 18.

4. Man's Alienation in Colonialism

RACIAL discrimination which is mediated by all the institutions of colonial society, determines the individual and social conduct of the colonized person both in his living together with the other colonized and in his relations with the colonist. The reasons for this can be found in the actual bi-partition of the colonial world characterized by domination and exploitation on the one hand, and in the imposition of a foreign culture and civilization, which is always a concomitant of oppression, on the other. The culture conflict to which the individual is exposed by growing up in a family of the traditional type, which conveys to him his own culture and religion, while at the same time being constantly confronted with the imported culture and its values, leads to uncertainty and anxiety in his behaviour. He adopts to a large extent the foreign norms suggested to him by the school, the press, the radio, books, films and publicity and in the countryside by the help of Christian missions.[1] This means at the same time that the racial stereotype of the colonized is interiorized by the victim himself. He reacts to this dilemma by mechanisms of compensation,

[1] Fanon quotes from the compositions of little black schoolgirls in Fort-de-France, who write, e.g., 'I like vacation because then I can run through the fields, breathe fresh air, and come home with *rosy* cheeks'. Frantz Fanon, *Black Skin White Masks*, trans. C. L. Markmann (London: MacGibbon & Kee, 1968), p. 162 fn.

overadaptation and finally self-hatred.[1] Indications of alienated behaviour on the part of the colonized can be discerned first of all in his attitude toward the institutions and norms of his own traditional society and those of the colonial, mostly industrialized society. His relation to his own as well as the foreign language must also be viewed from this angle. But the colonial situation determines interpersonal relations even in their most intimate aspects: the sexuai behaviour of the colonized who live in close social contact with the colonial power, assumes specific features conditioned by colonial racism. Psychosomatic illnesses and an abnormally high crime rate may be considered as evidence of this.

(A) THE ATTITUDE OF THE COLONIZED TOWARD CULTURE AND TECHNOLOGICAL PROGRESS

Fanon deals with the ambivalent attitude of the colonized toward both their own and the foreign culture and civilization in various studies and from different points of view. Traditional social institutions such as local assemblies or tribunals were reduced to utter ineffectiveness by colonialism. Controlled by the colonial administration and presided over by collaborationists, they have become a mere farce.[2] The history of the country is in serious danger of sinking into oblivion as the information media keep dinning into everybody's ear that history happens only in

---

[1] 'He (the colonized) is a marginal man moving from one world to the next, rejecting and despising in turn the one he has just left or turning violently against the one into which he is increasingly integrated but where nonetheless he still feels like a stranger'; Albert Meister, *L'Afrique peut-elle partir?* (Paris: Editions du Seuil, 1966), p. 127. Also see in this connection Gustav Jahoda's study, *White Man.* (London: O.U.P., 1961) especially chapter 8,. 'Psychological Reactions.

[2] See the description of a Kabyle village assembly during the Algerian revolution in Mouloud Mammeri's novel, *L'opium et le bâton* (Paris: Plon 1965).

Europe:[1] '... the history which he (the colonizer) writes is not the history of the country which he plunders but the history of his own nation in regard to all that she skims off, all that she violates and starves.'[2] Traditional rites and customs have long lost their living content. Their contact with colonialism has deprived them of their original functions and often changed them to mere escape mechanisms. In order to flee from the pressures of colonial reality, the natives take refuge in weird myths, spirit possession and ecstatic dances: 'The atmosphere of myth and magic frightens me and so takes on an undoubted reality. By terrifying me, it integrates me in the traditions and the history of my district or of my tribe, and at the same time it reassures me, it gives me a status, as it were an identification paper'.[3] Even the bloody tribal feuds can only be explained in this manner. 'By throwing himself with all his force into the *vendetta*, the native tries to persuade himself that colonialism does not exist, that everything is going on as before, that history continues.'[4] This vehement, distressed flight into old traditions and religious customs, this obsessive reintegration of the individual into structures which have long been deprived of their vital functions has an obvious character of regression. However, Fanon fails to acknowledge in his analysis that religious movements in the colonies may also have

---

1 Everything seems to have happened elsewhere: his (the colonized's) country and himself are either thin air or only exist in relation to the Gauls, the Franks or the River Marne, in relation to what he is not: to Christianity, while he is not a Christian, and to the Western world, which ends right in front of him ...' A. Memmi, *Portrait du colonisé, précédé du portrait du colonisateur* (Paris: Pauvert 1966), p. 142

2 Frantz Fanon, *The Wretched of the Earth*, trans. C. Farrington (London: MacGibbon & Kee, 1965), p. 41.

3 Fanon, *The Wretched*, p. 44.

4 ibid., p. 43.

progressive anti-colonial tendencies.[1] In such cases the traditional religion is not practiced in its original form but replaced by a syncretized form of the old religions and imported Christianity. A typical example is Kimbangism in the Congo, which rejects Christ as the colonial God and substitutes its own black prophets for him in the trinitarian formula, 'in the name of the father, of Simon Kimbangu and of André Matsua'. Laternari,[2] while pointing out the escapist character of such movements, also emphasizes the fact that they should be viewed as preliminary stages of an organized anti-colonial opposition: 'The very nature of these reform movements . . . shows a feature characteristic of the indigenous cultures. A cultural tradition, matured by the experience of misery and all kinds of subjection, prompts these cultures to react against oppression, anxiety and frustration first and foremost in the religious field, and only then on the organisational and political level'.[3] At least during the first phase of the anti-colonial struggle the new messianic religions which have been appearing in many colonies of Africa, Latin America and Asia, have a progressive character in so far as by preaching the Africanization or adaptation of Christian doctrines to local conditions they fan the embers of a nascent nationalism and present the struggle against colonialism as a struggle against the deformations of colonial Christianity.

Together with the obsessive clinging to the traditional world, which has been stagnating under the impact of colonialism, we find a wholesale rejection of the colonial civilization including technological

---

[1] We can only criticize Fanon with some reservations since his analysis is based on the example of Islam. Our own reflections which follow refer to the contact between Christian and animist religions and should, therefore, be compared to Fanon's general conclusions.

[2] Vittorio Laternari, *Les mouvements religieux des peuples opprimés*, 'Les Textes à l'appui', (Paris: Maspero, 1962).

[3] ibid., pp. 17–18.

progress. It becomes impossible for the colonized to distinguish between institutions having a purely repressive function and those that might be conducive to their general progress since any measure of a partially progressive nature also entails an effective economic exploitation of their labour force and is at the same time compromised by racism and oppression. 'The truth objectively expressed is constantly vitiated by the lie of the colonial situation.'[1]

The partial rationality of individual institutions and measures within the irrational whole of the colonial system baffles the colonized and brings about their ambivalent attitude toward all norms and institutions of the system. Thus they view modern medicine[2] from the same ambivalent angle. Even though its positive results may be self-evident, they still tend to reject or sabotage it: 'Introduced into Algeria at the same time as racialism and humiliation, Western medical science, being part of the oppressive system, has provoked in the native an ambivalent attitude'.[3] This attitude is not sufficiently explained by the traditional inhibitions of a backward population, although in many traditional societies the practice of medicine as a form of magic is identical with the exercise of political power, which is doubtless a pointer to the

1 Frantz Fanon, *Studies in a Dying Colonialism*, intr. Adolfo Gilly, trans. Haakon Chevalier, (New York: Monthly Review Press, 1965), p. 128.

2 ibid, chapter 5, 'Medicine and Colonialism'. Another example thoroughly analyzed by Fanon is the attitude of the native population toward the radio. Initially it is boycotted as the voice of the oppressor but as soon as the liberation movement has set up its own broadcasting station, the situation changes. The technical instrument imported by the colonizer is adapted to become an important weapon in the struggle against the colonial power: 'First of all, there was the stripping from the instrument of its traditional burden of taboos and prohibitions. Progressively the instrument not only acquired a category of neutrality, but was endowed with a positive coefficient'. ibid., p. 44. Also see chapter 2, 'This is the Voice of Algeria,' pp. 69–97.

3 ibid., p. 121. In his study of the Belgian Congo Merlier arrives at very similar results: 'The Congolese peasants show a similarly hostile attitude toward colonial medicine'. *Le Congo de la colonisation belge à l'indépendance*, (Paris: F. Maspero, 1962), p. 62.

motivations, especially of influential groups opting for resistance: by their acceptance of modern medicine they would cut themselves off from the traditional centres of power. The other explanation, which stresses the fact that the medical doctors are actually agents of colonialism as evidenced, e.g., by their 'looking after' prisoners subjected to torture or by never appearing without a police escort even when coming to villages on harmless health visits, is likewise not fully adequate. Fanon interprets this attitude which to all intents and purposes is inimical to progress, as an unconscious defensive reaction on the part of the colonized who rejects colonialism in its entirety and is afraid of manifesting his tacit approval of oppression by making even the slightest concession. The acceptance of isolated measures is in fact misconstrued by the colonial master as a confirmation and recognition of the system as a whole, and it is exploited propagandistically. 'He (the colonized) rejected doctors, schoolteachers, engineers, parachutists, all in one lump.'[1]

In the same measure as the individual's contact with the colonial power and its institutions grow closer, he increasingly undergoes processes of alienation. He becomes more and more uncertain with regard to the conduct he should adopt. His potential of revolutionary resistance decreases proportionately, since his acceptance of the colonialist ideology prevents him from realizing the causes of alienation.[2] With this hypothesis as his starting-point, Fanon interprets the tendency of the colonized to reject imported technology as distrust of an instrument capable of increasing the degree of exploitation through rationalization, and at the same time as an expression of inarticulate

---

1 Fanon, *Studies*, p. 123.

2 This interpretation helps to explain Fanon's evaluation of the various classes: Compared with other classes of society, the rural masses, whom he considers the only revolutionary force in the countries of the Third World, live at a greater distance from the colonial power.

and unorganized political resistance against colonialism. Fanon's thesis is confirmed by his individual studies of the Algerian revolution.

(B) THE COLONIZED AND LANGUAGE

In addition to the Christian missions the colonial school system is one of the most important institutions assuring a close personal contact with the indigenous population and creating a greater distance between the colonized and his own traditions and systems of reference. It is instrumental in transforming Africans into 'white Negroes', to borrow Fanon's own phrase. It is true that only few of the colonized ever have the opportunity of attending a colonial school, but it is just this minority on which devolve the leading roles in the colonial revolution and immediately after independence.[1] At school the children learn, together with the language of the colonizer, the ideological connotations of the various words, in particular the value judgments attached to the antonyms black and white. They increasingly use expressions, proverbs and parables aimed at their own origin, and disparaging it.[2] In most cases the children in the course of their studies identify with what they learn, and apply the racial stereotype, first, to other blacks and eventually, after the traumatic realization that they are black

---

1 In some colonies there existed at the same time indigenous educational systems which were tolerated by the colonial authorities, although viewed with some distrust, but closed immediately at the beginning of nationalist uprisings. Cases in point are the autonomous Kikuyu schools in Kenya, closed at the beginning of the Mau-Mau rebellion, and the Koranic schools in Algeria, closed down in the course of the war of liberation.

2 'Let (the colonial) open his mouth and he condemns himself, except in so much as he sets himself to destroy the hierarchy. And if he destroys it in French, he poeticizes already; let one imagine the strange savour which terms such as "the blackness of innocence" or the "shadows of virtue" would have for us,. J. P. Sartre, *Black Orpheus*, trans. S. W. Allen (Paris: Présence Africaine, 1964), p. 27.

too, even to themselves.[1] Jahoda has analyzed the textbooks of Ghanaian schoolchildren, which are exclusively written by Europeans. In these books, in particular in the ones specifically written for Africans, the Europeans appear only in a favourable light. The qualities allegedly lacking in Africans are strongly emphasized and glorified:

> School children were thus led to internalize a set of values that were in some crucial respects at variance with those to which they were exposed in their home evironment; values which they heard were characteristic of Europeans and had made them as strong, wise, and powerful as they were. At the same time the children could not help being aware that these virtues were not practiced by their own family and neighbours. This, naturally, was merely an indirect way of suggesting inferiority.[2]

Fanon also attributes great importance to extra-scholastic institutions and media which play a role in the socialization process. Under the heading of 'collective catharsis' he studies extensively the influence of comic strips, whose friend/enemy clichés are exclusively conceived for white children. Thus a heavy price has to be paid for the escape from illiteracy: 'The colonized is only saved from illiteracy to find himself on the horns of a new dilemma: linguistic dualism—if he has this chance at all.'[3] But learning the language of the colonizer is a prerequisite for any

---

[1] Fanon describes the racism of Antilles Negroes against black Africans, which is in turn adopted by the black Africans themselves as defined by the 'self-fulfilling prophecy'. Thus it occurs quite frequently that black Africans in France learn Creole in order to pass as West Indians and make a 'better impression'. See Fanon, 'West Indians and Africans', in *Toward the African Revolution*, trans. H. Chevalier (New York: Monthly Review Press, 1967), pp. 17–27.

[2] Jahoda, *White Man*, pp. 122–123, also p. 99. In another context Jahoda analyzes the reaction of African cinema-goers to films set in Africa: '. . . they did *not* identify with the Africans on the screen, but adopted to them something of the attitude European audiences would adopt; in other words they were apt to judge fellow-Africans by white standards of "civilized" behaviour'. ibid., p. 105.

[3] Memmi, *Portrait du Colonisé*, p. 143.

social advancement, for the mother tongue either has always only been passed on orally, or it has been deprived of its written form and is completely banned from public life: from the administration, postal services and transport to as well as from, e.g., invoices, train schedules or road-signs. The colonized who has no opportunity of learning the foreign language is a stranger in his own country. Fanon investigates the problem with reference to the Caribbean: 'The Negro of the Antilles will be proportionately whiter—that is, he will come closer to being a real human being—in direct ratio to his mastery of the French language'.[1] The bourgeoisie of the Antilles, e.g., does not speak Creole, which their children are taught to look down upon at school. Only a person capable of expressing himself in good French is feared and respected, albeit only by his equals. Both his colonial master and Europeans from the metropolis for whose recognition the colonized has been striving by learning their language, show him their contempt. Irrespective of his proficiency in the language they continue using a pidginized type of language when speaking to him (*parler petit-nègre*).

These observations are only true of the sphere of influence of French colonialism. The Africans in the former British colonies speak an Africanized form of English which only externally bears some resemblance to *petit-nègre*. This version of English is clearly distinguishable from British English. However, in contrast to *petit-nègre*, which is only a result of the limited linguistic proficiency and expressiveness of the colonized, both in the Frenchman's mind and in the colonized's own estimation, this African Nationality is also retained in social contact with Europeans, although the British-educated African would not be hard put to speak the King's English in a phonetically correct manner.

---

[1] Fanon, *Black Skin*, p. 18.

These differences, which are of great significance in a study of phenomena of alienation specifically arising from the colonial situation, can be explained, although in a somewhat summary fashion, by analyzing the British and French colonial policies with their different basic orientation. French assimilation policy unceasingly inculcated into the colonized the idea that he could only escape his underprivileged position by wholly adopting French culture and virtually gave him no opportunity of reinterpreting its form and content according to his own mental outlook. Even Negritude in its rebellious stance remained entirely within the pale of existing modes of thought and expression. The British policy of 'indirect rule', on the other hand, created a clearcut division from the onset, institutionalizing the social distance and the purported difference existing between the colonial overlord and the colonized, both on the administrative and the cultural level. The African was compelled to seek his chance for self-assertion and advancement in the colonial hierarchy not just by simply imitating the English way of life but also by consciously developing his faculties of self-reliance, e.g., by freely adapting imported elements of British culture and civilization and thus bending them to new requirements.

As a rule, it can be said that the relation of the colonized toward the language of the colonial dominator is ambivalent. He covets and respects it as a means of social climbing, while at the same time hating and dreading it as an instrument of colonial rule. The illiterates especially know it only in the form of commands or insults: 'Every French expression referring to the Algerian had a humiliating content. Every French speech heard was an order, a threat, or an insult'.[1] Fanon mentions that before the war of liberation Algerians suffering from clouding of intellectual

[1] Fanon, *Studies*, p. 89.

or sensory perception would in their hallucinations hear aggressive, hostile voices speaking French. He observed that the Algerians' attitude toward the French colonial language changed in the same measure as French was introduced on the FLN radio and added to its previously bilingual broadcasts in Arabic and Kabyle: 'The broadcasting in French of the programs of *Fighting Algeria* was to liberate the enemy language from its historic meanings'.[1] In psychopathology he could detect similar changes. Algerian patients suffering from hallucinations indicated that the French voices they heard were becoming less and less aggressive and frequently even assumed a friendly character of protection and support.

At this juncture we venture to point to the character of language as an instrument of domination tied to a class, even though the material available in our case does not allow any definitive conclusions. In view of the middle class background of Europeans in the colonies,[2] to which is frequently added their status as ex-servicemen, as we have previously pointed out, one could formulate the hypothesis that the colonized only get acquainted with a class-specific variant of the European language concerned. In dealing with Alfredo Nicefero's linguistic theory Walter Benjamin briefly discusses this aspect of language and criticizes linguistics for having hitherto neglected the connection between the structure of a given society and its language:[3] 'Traditional linguistics . . . has shown little

---

[1] ibid., p. 80.

[2] In his study of Ghana, Jahoda points out that the European norms adopted by Africans are typical of the British middle class: 'The conflict was intensified by the fact that the norms internalized were not only British, but somewhat old-fashioned British middle class ones". Jahoda, *White Man*, p. 123, also p. 102.

[3] See in this connection also Basil Bernstein, 'Soziokulturelle Determinaten des Lernens, mit besonderer Berücksichtigung der Rolle der Sprache', in *Soziologie der Schule*, special issue no. 4 of *Kölner Zeitschrift für Soziologie und Sozialpsychologie*, Cologne (1959). Bernstein analyzes the class-specific differences in the language of the middle and lower classes, drawing his examples from British school children.

inclination to investigate the sociological problems inherent in the languages of oppressed peoples ...'[1] Benjamin's criticism of linguistics is still valid today. In general research in the sociology of language tends to disregard completely the character of language as a phenomenon of domination.[2] Even when colonialism itself is under discussion, only quantitative changes in the languages concerned are subjected to scrutiny.[3]

Many politicians and writers from countries which formerly were, or still are, colonies find themselves confronted with the dilemma of being unable to make themselves generally understood except in the language of the colonizers. This is due to the great variety of local languages and dialects, often the result of the arbitrary delimitation of territories during the colonial era. 'The colonist rises between the colonials to be the eternal mediator; he is there, always there, even though absent, in the most secret councils'.[4]

---

[1] Walter Benjamin, 'Problem der Sprachsoziologie', in *Angelus Novus*, (Frankfurt a. M.: Suhrkamp (1966), pp. 77–78.

[2] Adam Schaff, who also attempts a critical assessment of linguistics, likewise pays scant attention to this aspect of language. For him as for others the influence of culture on language is 'a typically linguistic problem calling for a linguist's expertise ...' Adam Schaff, *Sprache und Erkenntniss* (Vienna, Europa Verlag, 1964), pp. 178-179.

[3] There is a possibility that class-specific speech not only mediates domination but even exercises it directly. It can be historically proved that languages rich in consonants tend to become gradually vocalized or adopted as *lingue franche* in their respective areas of domination. But the richer in vowels a language becomes, the greater are its handicaps as a vehicle of communication, the more it is bound to be controlled by the ear and to hinder the development of action-oriented aptitudes in the socialization process of the individual. See Christian Doermer, *Sprechphysiologie, Charakter und Herrschaft*, 1969.

[4] Sartre, *Black Orpheus*, pp. 22–23. The following poem by the Haitian poet Léon Laleau expresses this dilemma: Ce coeur obsédant qui ne correspond, pas à mon langage, ou à mes coutumes,/Et sur lequel mordent, comme un crampon,/Des sentiments d'emprunt et des coutumes/d'Europe, sentez-vous cette souffrance,/Et ce désespoir à nul autre égal/d'apprivoiser avec des mots de France/ce coeur qui m'est venu du Sénégal. Reprinted in L. S. Senghor, *Anthologie de la nouvelle poésie nègre et malgache* (Paris: Presses Universitaires de France, 1948), 2nd ed. 1969. Free translation: Behold this heart at variance/with my speech, my way of life/and lacerated by the barbs/ of borrowed feelings/ from the white man's arsenal./ Who can bear/ the desolation and despair/ befalling him who with the words of France/attempts to tame his heart from Senegal?

The enforced use of the foreign language modifies the very meaning of speech. The European language, which has developed in an altogether different historical context, cannot adequately express the experience of the colonized, which is nourished from the sources of his own history.

> Human beings are products of history not only in their bearing and their way of dressing, their stature as well as their mentality, but also in their manner of seeing and hearing, which cannot be dissociated from the process of social life as it has developed over the millenia. The facts presented to us by our senses are performed in two ways: on the one hand by the historical character of the object perceived, and on the other, by the historical character of the organ of perception.[1]

There are numerous indications that in the long run the European languages will be adapted and restructured in such a way that the traditional ideological content of individual words will slowly be drained of its original meaning or even superseded by a new content. The affinity existing between Negritude poetry and surrealism is not purely coincidental; the necessity of expressing oneself in the colonial language turns out to be a virtue; conventional concepts with heavy ideological overtones are re-interpreted or changed into their opposites.

Kateb Yacine, one of the most outstanding Algerian writers, in his novel, *Le polygone étoilé*, analyzes the alienation brought about by the break with his mother tongue, Arabic, a theme pervading all his novels and plays written in French:

> I have never ceased . . . to feel deep down within myself this second breaking of the umbilical cord, this inner exile which brought the schoolboy and his mother closer together only to tear them apart a bit more each time . . . with a banned language reproachfully shivering, secretly in

---

[1] Max Horkheimer, 'Traditionelle und kritische Theorie', in *Zeitschrift für Sozialforschung*, Year 6, no. 2, Paris (1937): 255.

agreement, an agreement as quickly broken as concluded. Thus I had lost my mother and her language at the same time, the only inalienable treasures—and yet alienated![1]

(c) THE COLONIZED AND SEXUALITY

Not only the social dealings of the colonized, which as a reaction to the norms and institutions of the colonial society reflect the alienation inherent in its economic conditions, but also his personal and sexual relations are alienated.[2] Not only the rare partnerships between blacks and whites are self-conscious and constrained but even the supposedly normal interpersonal relations among the colonized are handicapped by their constant confrontation with racial norms modelled on European ideals. The relationship with a white partner is the common ideal, while relationships with coloured partners are given a comparatively low rating. In mulattoes the desire to become lighter by a liaison with a white person sometimes even takes on grotesque proportions.

Fanon starts from the assumption that untrammelled sexual relations no longer encumbered by racial complexes will not become possible until the colonized have overcome the obsession of always comparing themselves to the white world: 'It is our problem to ascertain to what extent authentic love will remain unattainable before one has purged oneself of that feeling of inferiority or that Adlerian

---

1 Kateb Yacine, *Le Polygone étoilé* (Paris: Editions du Seuil, 1966), pp. 181–182

2 Even in capitalist industrial societies which have reached an advanced stage of development the sexual behaviour of man, conditioned as it is by the exchange character of social relations in general, is an aspect particularly well suited to demonstrate the fact of his alienation: 'Whether it represents the crowning glory of social success or an escape from prevailing conditions, whether it is an expression of purchasing power or of the lack of it, sexuality is only an epiphenomenon of a sociological fact . . . We are therefore dealing with a sexuality of frustration; the capitalist is frustrated by the money for the sake of which he is being "loved", the proletarian is frustrated by the wretchedness of his position, which is due to his lack of resources'. Jean Brun, 'Aliénation et sexualité', in *Esprit*, no. 11. Paris (1960): 1811.

exaltation, that overcompensation, which seem to be the indices of the black *Weltanschauung*.'[1] With the aid of Alfred Adler's categories Fanon tries to elucidate the mechanism of comparison. But he only uses these categories for describing the phenomenon, while his conclusions transcend the psychological frame of reference and aim at radical social changes. Any analysis of colonial conditions, including their psychological implications, exceeds the scope of psychoanalysis as it demands more than just a genetic explanation pertaining to an individual. Fanon does not intend to cure individual neuroses through insight; what he is concerned with is to elucidate the psychogenic conditions of a collective neurosis in order to remove it together with its formative causes.

At the centre of Adler's individual psychology is the assumption that man in his early childhood, through contacts with other human beings, undergoes enduring experiences which cause inferiority complexes (e.g., submission to an adult, experiences of inadequacy owing to false education, atrophied development of an organ, etc.). The attempt to react to such experiences through compensation may lead to psychoneuroses which in most cases can be cured with the aid of pedagogical methods by integrating the individual into a group.[2] Fanon concurs with the Adlerian analysis in so far as the Negro, or the colonized, tends to compare himself with the image of the white man, which results in feelings of submission and inferiority complexes: 'The Negro is comparison. There is the first truth. He is comparison: that is, he is constantly preoccupied with self-evaluation and with the ego-ideal. Whenever he comes into contact with someone else, the question of value, of merit, arises'.[3] However,

---

1 Fanon, *Black Skin*, p. 42.

2 Alfred Adler, *Über den nervösen Charakter* (Wiesbaden: J. F. Bergmann, 1912).

3 Fanon, *Black Skin*, p. 211.

the special conditions of colonialism are not without consequences for the process of socialization of the individual, which modify the Adlerian conception. While according to Adler human beings in general try to compensate their inferiority complexes by manifesting a fictitious superiority *vis-à-vis* others, two dimensions of conduct reflecting the Manichean structure of colonial society have to be taken into account in the colonized: he does not compensate his inferiority complexes with the colonial master, who is too powerful and dreaded, but by venting his feelings on the colonized who are themselves exposed to similar pressures: 'The Martinican does not compare himself with the white man *qua* father, leader, God; he compares himself with his fellow against the pattern of the white man'.[1] Adler's psychology of the individual cannot do justice to colonial problems, which are essentially social problems: 'It is not just this or that Antillean who embodies the neurotic formation, but all Antilleans. Antillean society is a neurotic society, a society of "comparison". Hence we are driven from the individual back to the social structure.'[2]

With the aid of this modified Adlerian approach Fanon discusses the sexual behaviour of the colonized. He describes the relationship of the coloured woman with the white man, and of the coloured man with the white woman, i.e., extreme cases of alienation within the colonial context, by drawing on three autobiographical novels; *Je suis Martiniquaise*, by Mayotte Capécia, *Nini*, by Abdoulaye Sadji, and *Un homme pareil aux autres*, by René Maran.[3] Interracial sexual contacts in particular seem to afford the colonized a solution to his problems, albeit only in the private sphere. In actual fact such problems, being the product

---

[1] ibid., p. 215.

[2] ibid., 213.

[3] See also chapter 2, 'The woman of colour and the white man', and chapter 3, 'The man of colour and the white woman'.

of objective conditions, do not allow of any subjective solution. Through her liaison with a white man the woman of colour finally wins admittance to the coveted world of the dominators; the man of colour by having a sexual relationship with a white woman takes revenge on the colonial master and at the same time proves that he is his equal, a member of the human race.[1] In the final analysis, however, this attitude only serves to corroborate the colonizer's value judgements by the very importance the colonized attaches to such exceptional situations, and consequently, race prejudice is given additional sanction. The colonized person himself is constantly confirmed in that type of behaviour only which through a display of inferiority complexes testifies to his fixation to the colonial master; 'In the man of colour there is a constant effort to run away from his own individuality, to annihilate his own presence. Whenever a man of colour protests, there is alienation'.[2]

The colonized man is handicapped in establishing contacts with his environment through his complexes and feelings of insecurity; by and by he becomes, in Fanon's phrase, the 'prisoner of an unbearable insularity'. Any possible way out of this solitude inevitably leads him into the white world. Fanon tries to explain this ego-restriction with reference to Anna Freud's theory: 'When (the ego) has become rigid or has already acquired an intolerance of pain and so is obsessionally fixated to a method of flight, such withdrawal is punished by impaired development. By abandoning one position after another it becomes one-sided, looses too many

[1] Fanon only wishes to underline the typical features discernible in such behaviour patterns without, however, claiming that they can be observed in *all* colonized people: 'Just as there was a touch of fraud in trying to deduce from the behaviour of Nini and Mayotte Capécia a general law of the behaviour of the black woman with the white man, there would be a similar lack of objectivity, I believe, in trying to extend the attitude of Veneuse (the hero of Maran's novel) to the man of colour as such'. Fanon, *Black Skin*, p. 81.

[2] ibid., p. 60.

interests and can show but a meagre achievement.'[1] Anna Freud describes ego-restriction as a method of avoiding unpleasure (*Unlust*) and considers it a stage in the normal development of the ego. Fanon on the other hand thinks that any form of ego-withdrawal in the colonized person is bound to have neurotic features as long as he requires white approval and is unable to compensate his withdrawal by other activities of the ego.[2] To illustrate his point he mentions the case of an educated Mulatto woman, a student.

> She says, "I do not like the Negro because he is savage. Not savage in a cannibal way, but lacking refinement". An abstract point of view. And when one points out to her that in this respect some black people may be her superiors, she falls back on their "ugliness". A factitious point of view. Faced with the proofs of a genuine black esthetic, she professes to be unable to understand it; one tries then to explain its canon to her; the wings of her nose flare, there is a sharp intake of breath, "she is free to choose her own husband". As a last resort, the appeal to subjectivity.[3]

(D) PSYCHOSOMATIC DISORDERS AND CRIME AS INDICES OF ALIENATION

The unusually frequent occurence of cases of psychosomatic disorder and a crime rate far above average both bear witness to the essentially pathological character of colonial society.[4] Fanon has investigated both pheno-

---

[1] Anna Freud, *The Ego and the Mechanism of Defence* (New York: International Universities Press, 1946), p. 111.

[2] Fanon's criticism here takes on fundamental significance. Whether ego-withdrawal can be termed a healthy phenomenon in the normal process of ego development is in fact a moot point.

[3] Fanon, *Black Skin*, pp. 58–59.

[4] We use Durkheim's term in this context, although with some reservations, since it expresses in a summary fashion what has hitherto been said about colonial society on the basis of unrelated observations. This term as used to describe the colonial situation is critically assessed by Meister, *L'Afrique*, pp. 145 ff.

mena, basing his case on the example of the North African colonies.[1]

The unceasing violent confrontation of the colonized person with the norms and institutions of the colonial system leaves its imprint on his personality structure and produces mechanisms of defense and processes of compensation in his psychic makeup. If the defense mechanisms collapse under extreme pressure, psychosomatic disorders ranging from general indispositions to manifest physical changes are the result: 'There is thus during this calm period of successful colonisation a regular and important mental pathology which is the direct product of oppression'.[2] Fanon uses the term *syndrome nord-africain* to designate the whole complex of insufficiently defined disorders with frequently changing symptoms which he came across in his work as a psychiatrist. The aspects of the case are always the same; the patient feels some vague pain which he is at first unable to localize until after a great deal of questioning he localizes it in the vicinity of the stomach. If the physician finally manages to detect a pathogenic focus, e.g., a stomach ulcer, and treats it successfully, the patient immediately discovers new symptoms, such as vertigo or headache. The doctor, mostly acting in accordance with the maxim, 'No symptom without a tangible somatic modification,' grows impatient since he is, of course, fully aware of the fact that North Africans 'are by nature lazy and unwilling to work'. In view of the large number of Arab patients 'simulating' diseases he finds himself confirmed in his prejudice: 'The medical staff discovers

[1] For further details on the problem of psychosomatic disorders see Fanon, 'The "North African syndrome", in *Toward the African Revolution*, pp. 3–16. On crime see Fanon, *The Wretched*, chap. 5, subsection entitled 'Criminal Impulses found in North Africans which have their origin in the National War of Liberation', pp. 238–251.

[2] Fanon, *The Wretched*, p. 204.

the existence of a North African syndrome. Not experimentally, but on the basis of an oral tradition. The North African takes his place in this asymptomatic syndrome and is automatically put down as undisciplined (cf. medical discipline), inconsequential (with reference to the law according to which every symptom implies a lesion), and insincere (he says he is suffering when we know there are no reasons for suffering).'[1] The cases of psychosomatic disorder, which occur even in the 'calm' periods of colonial administration, increase considerably in number during a colonial war.[2] Fanon lists the following psychiatric symptoms of psychosomatic illnesses which he treated during the Algerian war: stomach ulcers, nephritic colics, menstruation trouble in women, intense sleeplessness caused by idiopathic tremors, hair turning white prematurely, paroxysmal tachycardias, and generalized contraction with muscular stiffness.

The disproportionately high crime rate recorded during the colonial period,[3] which is interpreted by racially prejudiced specialists on colonial affairs as a result of physiological deficiencies in the natives, tends to drop during the colonial war and remains at a normal level after independence. Fanon explains the criminality of the colonized, which is rarely directed against the colonizer but primarily against his own fellows, as an uncontrolled eruption of pent-up aggressivity built up over long periods of unbearable pressure. During the pre-revolutionary phase such aggressions are not yet aimed at the colonizer, whose military superiority makes him appear unassailable, but are

---

[1] Fanon, *Toward the African Revolution*, pp. 9–10.

[2] In a chapter entitled 'Colonial War and Mental Disorders', Fanon analyses the repercussions of torture, referring to individual cases of torturers as well as their victims. See *The Wretched*, pp. 201–251.

[3] Again Fanon only deals extensively with the countries of the Magrab; comparative figures for East Africa, which show that the situation there is identical, are given by Meister, *L'Afrique*, p. 144.

discharged in unpolitical behaviour patterns of avoidance such as cultic rituals, dances, spirit possession or criminal acts. This tension is reflected in the dreams of the colonized: 'The native is being hemmed in; apartheid is simply one form of the division into compartments of the colonial world. The first thing which the native learns is to stay in his place, and not to go beyond certain limits. This is why the dreams of the native are always of muscular prowess; his dreams are of action and of aggression'.[1] The world of the dominator, guarded by the army and the police, is coveted and hated at the same time: 'The native is a persecuted person whose permanent dream is to become the persecutor'.[2] As a rule, however, his direct contacts with the representatives of the colonial power are rare; wherever the colonized, with his nerves on edge, meets other people, be it at work, in his closely packed lodgings, at the grocer's where he still owes money, he meets people who like himself are under the colonizer's heel: mirror images of his own misery. It is on them that he vents his hatred, it is them that he dares to assault as long as he is too frightened or apathetic to revolt against the colonizer himself: 'While the settler or the policeman has the right the live-long day to strike the native, to insult him and to make him crawl to them, you will see the native reaching for his knife at the slightest hostile or aggressive glance cast on him by another native; for the last resort of the native is to defend his personality *vis-à-vis* his brother'.[3] Fanon considers such criminal acts as collective 'behaviour patterns of avoidance'.[4]

---

[1] Fanon, *The Wretched*, p. 41.
[2] ibid., p. 42.
[3] ibid., p. 43. Sartre describes the same phenomenon as an example of alienated behaviour enforced by the Manichean structure of colonial society. See *Critique de la raison dialectique* (Paris: Gallimard 1960), p. 685.
[4] Fanon, *The Wretched*, p. 43.

In these interpretations we can already perceive in outline the basic conception of Fanon's theory of violence; by relaying the pressure of the colonial system under which he suffers and aiming it at his fellow-sufferers, the colonized man acts against his own interests, that is to say, in an alienated manner. But if popular resistance is politicized and organized in such a way as to lead to acts of violence against the true enemy—the colonizer—violence loses its criminal character: it now becomes emancipatory and. hence, a potential instrument of disalienation.

Criminal acts are encouraged by the fact that to the colonized the norms, codes of conduct and, consequently, the laws of the colonial master are just empty formulas.[1] They never apply to him, so why should he conform to them? '...Honour, dignity and respect for the given word can only manifest themselves in the framework of national and international homogeneity. From the moment that you and your like are liquidated like so many dogs, you have no other resource but to use all and every means to regain your importance as a man'.[2] This quotation points to an essential constitutive element of society, which is a central notion of Durkheim's sociology: the 'non-contractual element of the contract'.[3] This element, which goes beyond the legally formulated contracts of individuals and guarantees the observation of social norms and conventions by its implicit character of constraint causes

---

[1] Fanon expounds the attitude of the colonized to work under the same aspect: 'And yet is it not the simple truth that under the colonial regime a *fellah* who is keen on his work or a negro who refuses to rest are nothing but pathological cases? The native's laziness is the conscious sabotage of the colonial machine . . . Under the colonial regime, what is true for the Arab and for the negro is that they should not lift their little finger nor in the slightest degree help the oppressor to sink his claws deeper into his prey'. Ibid., p. 239

[2] ibid.

[3] This notion was first defined by Durkheim in his work, *Montesquieu et Rousseau*. Cf. René König in his introduction to Emile Durkheim, *Die Regeln der soziologischen Methode* (Neuwied: 1961), p. 33 (German edition of *Les Règles de la méthode sociologique*. Paris 1895).

the cohesion of a society or a social estate.[1] It is only the non-contractual element of the contract which gives contractual agreements between individuals among themselves, and between individuals and social institutions, meaning and substance. Through this element individual arbitrariness finds its limitations which, although reflected in laws in a general way, are not altogether congruous with them. The character of constraint of all forms of social life, which Durkheim here tries to establish, offers the individual a guarantee, over and above all normative guidelines, that his actions and claims will meet with an adequate response. The individual is thus enabled to find his bearings in society. For Durkheim, the non-contractual element of the contract in a society whose exchanges are based on the division of labour is assured by its organic solidarity. This means that in such a society a satisfactory consensus for all its members is arrived at by a rational division of labour. It is doubtful whether the same integrative element can be at work in a society kept together by mere coercion.[2] All indications point to the conclusion that in the colonial system, the social cohesion of which can only be brought about by the threat of repression, the non-contractual element of the contract is totally absent in the social relations between colonizer and colonized, but likewise in the mutual relations of the colonized.

The disproportionately high crime rate in the colonial society can thus be ascribed to its pathological state in Durkheim's sense.[3] The economic and social bases of

---

[1] ... even where society relies most completely upon the division of labour, it does not become a jumble of juxtaposed atoms, between which it can establish only external, transient contacts. Rather the members are united by ties which extend deeper and far beyond the short moments during which the exchange is made'. Emile Durkheim, *The Division of Labour in Society* (1893), (Glencoe, Ill.: The Free Press, 1933), p. 227.

[2] In this context it is of great importance to appreciate the fact that social relations in colonial societies are not based on economic exchange.

[3] A. Meister refers to the "pathologie sociale" as the exclusive cause of the high incidence of crime in the East African colonies, *L'Afrique*, p. 144 ff.

traditional society have been destroyed, and no attempt has been made to replace them with adequate new structures since the colonial economy is solely geared to the needs of the metropolis. The colonized has been torn away from his old conditions of production and their normative framework, without, however being integrated into the colonial society. His criminality can be interpreted as a reaction to the resultant state of economic disorientation. Fanon draws on the Algerian case to analyse the effects colonialism has on the colonized, but his conclusions are of general applicability: 'The Algerian's criminality, his impulsivity and the violence of his murders are therefore not the consequence of the organization of his nervous system nor of characterial originality, but the direct product of the colonial situation'.[1]

The interpretation of the phenomena under discussion leads us to the general problem of a scientific investigation of colonialism. Fanon's analysis shows that only an inter-disciplinary approach embracing psychological, sociological and economic methods of interpretation can do justice to the cluster of problems which is colonialism. What difficulties a purely ethnological approach to the study of these countries may be confronted with has been amply demonstrated in the past; most ethnologists did not realize that traditional societies had been changing under colonial influence, even though their outward forms might have remained the same. Even regions which were spared any direct colonization nevertheless succumbed to colonial pressure in the long run, e.g., when their trade was drawn into the sphere of influence of a colonial power, or when they were declared a nature reserve and thus reduced to stagnation. Another 'scientific' method is the apologetic mode of explanation based on natural science

---

[1] Fanon, *The Wretched*, p. 250.

which claims that the phenomena produced by colonialism are in actual fact natural constants. This method is already sufficiently discredited and therefore need not concern us further. A purely psychological or psychoanalytical approach would likewise be inadequate. Its major drawbacks are of a methodological nature: to what extent can categories developed for a study of individuals living in a capitalist, industrial society with its own specific family structures be applied to a colonial society? Fanon himself is unable to give an unequivocal answer to this question. Although he makes use of such categories, he points out that they are only of limited usefulness and have to be reinterpreted in the light of colonial conditions. His own clinical experiences in the field of social therapy had taught him that curative methods tried out on Europeans would fail utterly when applied to Arab patients;[1] only when he had adapted the methods of social therapy to the actual social conditions of the Arab colonial country did he achieve positive results.

We have analysed the comportment of colonized people as the expression of a specific form of alienation resulting from the conditions of colonial domination and exploitation. From the interpretation of these phenomena Fanon's political theory draws the concept of a violent struggle for emancipation, which is to create the conditions conducive to a process of dis-alienation. But first we want to discuss briefly the ideology of *negritude*, which by invoking the authenticity of colonized man gives a direct answer to the colonial ideology of white superiority.

---

[1] See F. Fanon and J. Azoulay, 'La socialthérapie dans un service d'hommes musulmans—Difficultés méthodologiques', in *L'Information Psychiatrique*, No. 9, Paris, (1954).

5. Negritude: An Antithesis of Colonial Racism

(A) HISTORICAL OVERVIEW

NEGRITUDE originated as a literary movement within the pale of French colonialism and is even today in the main restricted to the former French colonies. Its influence makes itself felt both in literature and in scholarly works.[1] The poem, *Cahier d'un retour au pays natal* by Aimé Césaire, published in *Volontés* in Paris in 1939, first went unnoticed. In it Césaire gave passionate expression to his feeling of revolt against white domination both political and cultural:

> Accomodez-vous de moi. Je ne m'accommode pas de vous!
> J'accepte . . . j'accepte . . . entièrement, sans réserve . . .
> ma race qu' aucune ablution d'hysope et de lys
> mêlée ne pourrait purifier
> ma race rongée de macules
> ma race raisin mûr pour pieds ivres
> ma reine des crachats et des lèpres
> ma reine des fouets et des scrofules
> ma reine des squasmes et des chloasmes . . .
> J'accepte. J'accepte[2]

---

[1] See in particular the historical studies of Cheikh Anta Diop and cf. in this context, E. Simon, 'La Négritude et les problèmes culturels de l'Afrique contemporaine' in *Présence Africaine*, Paris (1963, 3e trimestre).

[2] Aimé Césaire, *Cahier d'un retour au pays natal*, bilingual ed. with English trans. by Emile Snyders (Paris: Présence Africaine, 1968), pp. 69, 113–115. English trans.: 'Take me as I am, I don't adapt to you!/I accept. I accept . . . totally,/without reserve . . ./My race which no ablution of hyssop or mixed lilies could purify/My race eaten by macula/My race ripe grape for drunken feet/My queen of spittle and lepers/My queen of whips and scrofula/My queen of squasms and chloasms . . ./I accept . . . I accept.

For the first time the French language here served as an instrument of liberation from the European mind. It was not until André Breton, interned in Martinique by the Vichy government, discovered in 1941 the journal, *Tropiques*, founded by Aimé Césaire and praised him as the renovator of surrealism that his name became known beyond the confines of the Antilles. During the Second World War Césaire and his friends in the journal, *Tropiques*, tried to rediscover Africa's past before the era of the slave trade. Later the journal *Présence Africaine*, published in Paris by Alioune Diop, became the most important organ of negritude. Apart from Aimé Césaire, Léopold S. Senghor is considered its most outstanding representative.

The growing awareness manifesting itself in negritude poetry is a reaction to colonial racism: since colonialism despises the colonized for belonging to another race, race and colour are now exalted and raised to the status of autonomous values. Furthermore, as the virtue of the oppressed, negritude stands up against any form of oppression, irrespective of where it rears its head:

> The first enemy of the glorification of negritude is the acceptance of this inferiority. The glorification of negritude shows that pride and dignity have been recovered in the face of the European claim to "lay down the law". But it does more, and this explains its generosity. It wants to offer a truth which has been forgotten by modern societies, mechanized and encumbered with artifice as they are.[1]

Its irrationality expressed in the exaltation of metaphysical values like the 'Black Soul' and a mystical communion with nature should not blind us to its inherent rational elements which are a manifestation

---

[1] Georges Balandier, *Ambiguous Africa*, trans. Helen Weaver (London: Chatto & Windus, 1966), pp. 247–48.

of the revolt against the fake rationality of capitalism. Historically speaking, the irrationality of negritude has its own functioning value for the criticism of colonialism: 'Black poetry has nothing in common with the effusions of the heart; it is functional, it answers a need which exactly defines it'.[1]

For negritude the 'Black Soul' is a symbol of the Negro carried away by force from his native Africa, who suffers in the 'cold cities' under white civilization and technology. The hope of merging entirely with the Black Soul and of becoming one with Africa (return to the native land) is the *leitmotiv* pervading the whole of its poetry. What colonialism has stigmatized as deficiencies in the colonized—the absence of any technological development resulting from a lack of rationality—now becomes a source of positive riches: the white man possesses instrumental knowledge, but with his tools he can only touch the surface of things, he is unable to penetrate to the sources of life itself.[2] Negritude, on the other hand, wishes to embrace life through sympathy. This metaphysic is interpreted by Sartre as 'an agricultural poetry (which) opposes

---

[1] Jean-Paul Sartre, *Black Orpheus*, trans. Samuel W. Allen (Paris: Présence Africaine, 1963), pp. 17–18.

[2] The contrast elaborated by negritude between the technological civilization of the whites organized along the lines of rationality and expediency, and the black soul abandoning itself to feeling and giving rise to true humanity, is reminiscent of the Bergsonian distinction between intelligence and intuition. However, the pansexual character of intuition in negritude poetry differs from Bergson's ascetic variety of intuition. At the same time it must be borne in mind that the notions of "rationality" and "irrationality" have a different meaning in the histories of philosophy of France and Germany: 'What appears in its most acute form in such models. . . would be the conflict of rationalist and irrationalist motives, as the official history of philosophy has it. Their position on the scale of values in France is, however, the inverse of what it is in Germany. In France rationalism is identified with progress, and irrationalism—the heritage of Romanticism—with the Restoration. But Valéry succeeds in merging the traditional element with the Cartesian rationalist one, and in undertaking the autocritique of Cartesianism in an irrationalist manner . . . The relationship between an untrammelled subjective rationality and the self-alienation of the subject did not escape his notice; neither did the connection between this tendency and totalitarianism'. Theodor W. Adorno, 'Valérys Abweichungen', in *Noten zur Literatur II*, (Frankfurt a.M.: Suhrkamp 1961), pp. 63–66.

itself here to an engineer's prose'.[1] Negritude bases its comprehension of the world on the black man's intimate union with nature. His relation to God and nature is conceived of in sexual terms: 'To dig, to plant, to eat, is to make love with nature'.[2] All manifestations of life are given a sexual significance; comprehension results from the physical contact and union with all living things, from the intuitive grasping of nature. The absurd blustering activity of the white man is contrasted with the deep knowledge of the blacks, drawn from suffering. Out of the passion of slavery and oppression lasting for centuries, derives a sense of mission to redeem the world, including the white man. The experience of suffering has a double meaning; its be-all and end-all is not mere passivity but it has an historical dimension; it aims at the abolition of suffering: 'Suffering carries within itself its own refusal; it is in essence refusal to suffer... it opens itself toward revolt and toward liberty'.[3]

The conception of nature on which negritude is based reveals its dependence on the colonial stereotype. It is in keeping with the exotic cliché of 'Africa's untouched nature' from which human beings were expelled to make room for the establishment of nature reserves. Man's sexual relation to nature expresses a relationship of dominance and submission which is not recognized as such. Negritude fails to distinguish between internal and external nature; it does not take into account the deformation of man's immanent nature which ought to be charged to colonial domination in the same way as the destruction of the environment. Neither does it show any awareness of the problem of dominating nature, which is, after all, a prerequisite of progress. Although its praise of irrationality implies a utopian

---

[1] Sartre, *Black Orpheus*, p. 44.
[2] ibid., p. 45.
[3] ibid., p. 55.

type of criticism with regard to an uninhibited domination of nature, it does not initiate any new attitude toward nature not solely obsessed with domination, such as might result from a lifelong experience of suffering.

> Through thinking, men move away from nature and put her at arm's length as something to be dominated . . . Thinking is suffused with illusion if it insists on denying its vital function of separation, dissociation and objectification. Any mystical union remains a mirage, an impotent, interiorized trace of a revolution betrayed. But by the fact that enlightenment is proved right in its conflict with hypostatized utopias and boldly proclaims the principle of domination through disunion, the rupture between subject and object which it declines to conceal becomes the index of the latter's untruth and of truth itself.[1]

(B) ANTI-RACIST RACISM

Negritude can thus only be understood as a reaction to the racist colonialist ideology of white superiority. By emphasizing black authenticity it turns against the cultural self-alienation of the colonized and instils in them an awareness of their own historical and cultural tradition which embraces an awareness of all deformations suffered at the hands of colonialism. However, this differentiated, historical concept of cultural tradition only applies to the early phase of negritude (e.g. Césaire). Later on, this historical dimension is lost altogether, the cultural tradition is made into a fetish and colonialism is viewed only as the temporary interruption of an otherwise continuous process. By implication homage is paid to colonialism for having imported a language and culture which makes it possible for negritude (more recently 'la Francophonie') to be formulated (e.g., Senghor).

---

1 T. W. Adorno and Max Horkheimer, *Dialektik der Aufklärung* (Amsterdam: Querido, 1947), p. 54. See the chapter on "The Concept of Enlightenment".

The concept of authenticity will here be interpreted in the way it has been used by Sartre,[1] in his analysis of the two possible forms of reaction to anti-Semitism on the part of Jews. The first possibility is that of the non-authentic Jew who is constantly haunted by the image others have of him: 'Whatever he does, the non-authentic Jew is pursued by his awareness of being Jewish. The very moment he attempts through his whole attitude to deny the traits ascribed to him, he is convinced that he rediscovers them in others and is in this wise saddled with them again'.[2] He may be compared to the colonized person full of complexes who tries in vain to turn European; he is the 'white Negro'. The authentic Jew on the other hand is conscious of his peculiarity; full of self-confidence he assumes his Jewishness without, however, being able to solve the problem of anti-Semitism in this way. 'The authentic Jew gives up the myth of universal man. He knows himself and assumes his position in history as an historical, a condemned being. No longer does he run away from himself, nor is he ashamed of his own people.'[3]

This authenticity as defined by Sartre, which is a first step on the way to disalienation, although it cannot abolish and supersede alienation altogether, is the essential element of negritude. The black man, colonized and humiliated as he is, now proudly refers to the very qualities which a colonial ideology had stigmatized as racial flaws in him:

> Je vous remercie mon Dieu,
> de m'avoir créé Noir,
> d'avoir fait de moi
> la somme de toutes les douleurs,

---

[1] Sartre, *Réflexions sur la question juive* (Paris: Gallimard 1954), pp. 129–132, 165–171.
[2] ibid., p. 129.
[3] ibid., p. 166.

mis sur ma tête,
le Monde.
Le blanc est une couleur de circonstance
Le noir la couleur de tous les jours
Et je porte le Monde depuis le premier soir.
Je suis content
de la forme de ma tête
fait pour porter le Monde.
Satisfait
de la forme de mon nez.[1]

In invoking his authenticity the colonized intellectual rejects the colonial stereotype and lends expression to his growing awareness and his feeling of revolt.

In analyzing the reaction of negritude to the racist ideology of colonialism we can distinguish three elements, which turn out to be true and false at the same time. They are true in their criticism of the deplorable state of colonial society by means of: (*a*) attacking its false rationality; (*b*) rebelling against the negation of their own history; and (*c*) revolting against racial humiliation.

But the same elements become false when ideologically hypostatized, i.e., when their negative, critical claims are transformed into positive values which no longer reflect their determination through history, and they appear as: (*a*) glorification of irrationality, anti-technological resentment; (*b*) unhistorical glorification of the precolonial past; and (*c*) eulogy of the 'African Personality', which is dangerously close to the stereotype of the 'noble savage'.

The progressive function of negritude and similar ideologies, such as appear, e.g., in the Arab countries in the guise of a reawakening of Islam, consists of the

---

1 Poem by Bernard B. Dadié, reprinted in *Anthologie africaine et malgache*, ed. C. Reygnault and L. Hughes (Paris: Editions Seghers, 1962), p. 156. Trans. 'I thank you, my Lord, for having created me black/for having made me/ the sum of all troubles/for having placed the world/upon my head.../White is the colour for special occasions/Black the workaday colour/I've been carrying the world from the outset/I am satisfied/with the form of my head/ made to carry the world/happy/with the form of my nose'.

negation of colonial racism and the recollection of one's own historical traditions which colonialism threatened to consign to eternal oblivion. But even this negative, revolutionary response to colonialism is deeply marked by what it rejects: it bears itself racist features. Sartrè rightly calls it 'an anti-racist racism'.[1] The relativity of negritude stems from the fact that it has to rely on the methods of colonial ideology to react against it; even in the act of negating colonialism it reproduces its features. A case in point is the historical theory of Cheikh Anta Diop. The European form of social organizaion is contrasted with an African one whose socioeconomic structures as well as cultural and moral norms are supposed to be diametrically opposed to those of the former: patriarchy vs. matriarchy; city-state vs. territorial state; individualism vs. collectivism; a war-like ideal of force vs. an ideal of peace, justice, and goodness ... etc.[2] 'This historical necessity in which the men of African culture find themselves, to racialise their claims and to speak more of African culture than of national culture, will tend to lead them up a blind alley.'[3]

The actual historical processes disprove negritude's claim to speak for and on behalf of all blacks. The concrete problems encountered by black people in America and Africa, respectively, differ widely. But even within Africa the development of individual countries shows marked differences. The South African writer, Ezekiel Mphahlele, pointing out the different approaches of British and French colonial policy, interprets negritude as a reaction to the French policy of assimilation: 'It is significant that it is not the African in British-settled territories—a product of "indirect

---

[1] Sartre, *Black Orpheus*, p. 59. This term is adopted by Fanon.

[2] See in particular Cheikh Anta Diop, *The Cultural Unity of Black Africa* (Paris: Présence Africaine, 1962), pp. 195–197.

[3] Frantz Fanon, *The Wretched of the Earth*, trans. C. Farrington (London: MacGibbon & Kee, 1965), p. 173.

rule" and one that has been left in his cultural habitat —who readily reaches out for his traditional past. It is rather the assimilated African, who has absorbed French culture, who is now passionately wanting to recapture his past'.[1]

In keeping with its historical function negritude must be understood as 'anti-racist racism', as the negative phase of a process. It is not an end in itself but a means in the liberation struggle of the colonized:

> In fact, negritude appears as the weak stage of a dialectical progression: the theoretical and practical affirmation of white supremacy is the thesis; the position of negritude as antithetical value is the moment of negativity. But this negative element is not sufficient in itself . . . it serves to prepare the way for the synthesis or the realization of the human society without racism. Thus negritude is dedicated to its own destruction, it is passage and not objective, means and not the ultimate goal.[2]

If its protagonists, unmindful of this process, insist on sticking to the positions reached, negritude loses its progressive character and becomes a smokescreen for reactionary politics, to which it is inclined *a priori* by virtue of its content. Everybody knows the bitterly sarcastic remark of the Senegalese patriots about the manoeuvrings of their president, Senghor: 'We have demanded that the higher posts should be given to Africans; and now Senghor is Africanizing the Europeans'.[3]

The transformation of negritude from a revolutionary movement to an ideology of the establishment becomes evident if we compare the poetry of Aimé Césaire with that of Léopold S. Senghor. In Césaire's poems negritude never loses its bearing on colonialism, it remains a means of the revolutionary struggle, 'My name: offended one; my first name: humiliated one;

---

[1] E. Mphahlele, *The African Image* (London: Faber and Faber, 1962), p. 25.
[2] Sartre, *Black Orpheus*, pp. 59–60.
[3] Fanon, *The Wretched*, p. 37.

my status: rebellious; my age: the stone-age'.[1] Senghor, on the other hand, develops negritude into a universalist philosophy which has a redeeming function for the whole of mankind. What for Césaire was simply the recognition of a state of affairs is for Senghor a state that still remains to be achieved. While Césaire insists on analysing the phenomena of alienation resulting from European influence and stresses, e.g., the ambiguous influence of European languages, Senghor praises French as the best of all possible languages and colonialism as a civilizing mission which is open to criticism only in some details:

> It was our *condition as colonized people* which imposed on us the language of the colonizer, or more precisely, the policy of *assimilation*. However, not all was bad in this policy which derived from the "immortal principles" of 1789. Unfortunately, these principles of the Revolution were not applied in full and without hypocrisy. But luckily they were applied in part, at least to such an extent that their virtues, among them French culture, were allowed to bear fruit.[2]

Mphahlele, the determined critic and political opponent of a negritude sunk to the level of an ideology, seizes upon such statements to unmask the reactionary function of negritude in interior policy: 'Furthermore, a number of the apostles (of negritude) are being deliberately or unwillingly dishonest . . . Senghor has quite recently sung praises to French culture, and is quite happy . . . to be, as all blacks are in Africa, a synthesis of Africa and Europe. So *negritude* remains the intellectual pastime of the governing *élite*, another aspect of what a French writer calls the "autocolonization of Africa"[3].

---

1 Césaire, *Les armes miraculeuses*, Paris: Gallimard, 1946), p. 133.
2 L. S. Senghor, 'Négritude et Civilisation de l'Universel' in *Présence Africaine*, Paris (2e trimestre, 1963).
3 E. Mphahlele, 'Replying Chinua Achebe' in *Transition*, no. 9, Kampala (1963), p. 7.

The element of disalienation, which was at one time negritude's basic objective, now fades out completely. On the contrary, negritude henceforth helps to perpetuate the state of alienation. 'He (the native poet) cannot go forward resolutely unless he first realizes the extent of his estrangement . . .'[1]

(c) NEGRITUDE AND NATIONAL CULTURE

Fanon, who passionately postulated authenticity and analyzed the function of negritude in the above-stated sense as both an historical and psychological necessity, at the same time always had certain misgivings about its irrational elements: 'Nevertheless, one had to distrust rhythm, earth-mother love, this mystic, carnal marriage of the group and the cosmos'.[2]

At a later stage, taking the experiences gained during the Algerian war of liberation as his point of departure, he formulated his criticism of negritude in connection with his analysis of national culture:

> It is around the peoples' struggles that African-Negro culture takes on substance, and not around songs, poems or folklore. Senghor, who is also a member of the Society of African Culture . . . is not afraid for his part either to give the order to his (UNO) delegation to support French proposals on Algeria. Adherence to African-Negro culture and to the cultural unity of Africa is arrived at in the first place by upholding unconditionally the people's struggle for freedom. No one can truly wish for the spread of African culture it he does not give practical support to the creation of the conditions necessary to the existence of that culture; in other words, to the liberation of the whole continent.[3]

---

[1] Fanon, *The Wretched*, p. 182. Cf. Herbert Marcuse, 'All liberation depends on the consciousness of servitude'. *One-Dimensional Man*, Studies in the Ideology of Advanced Industrial Society (London: Routledge & Kegan Paul, 1964), p. 7.

[2] Frantz Fanon, *Black Skin White Masks*, trans. C. L. Markmann (London: MacGibbon and Kee, 1968), p. 125.

[3] Fanon, *The Wretched*, p. 189.

He criticizes the established philosophy of negritude for trying unhistorically to fabricate a black consciousness at a time when the colonial revolutions show that the 'Negro' is ceasing to exist. According to Fanon the writer's falling back on the past only has a meaning if it is linked in a concrete manner with present-day realities; otherwise culture remains mere folklore. As long as a country is not yet truly independent, any cultural action must be of a militant nature since it is first a matter of creating the very basis of a national culture:[1] 'To fight for national culture means in the first place to fight for the liberation of the nation, that material keystone which makes the building of a culture possible. There is no other fight for culture which can develop apart from the popular struggle'.[2] The concept of the nation as employed by Fanon has nothing in common with the narrow categories of the nation state. He uses this concept to circumscribe the national unity which has issued forth from the solidary liberation struggle of an oppressed people. It is not possible to speak of a nation and a national culture in this sense until a free, independent society determined by the interests and needs of the people has been created. Fanon thus considers all signs of solidarity among the oppressed, which only knows one objective, namely liberation, as expressions of a nascent national culture.

As a response to the generalizing colonial stereotype of the 'wild Africa' the established philosophy of negritude remains generally as vague as the stereotype itself. The concrete needs and struggles of the various African countries are dwarfed by the importance

---

1 Ezekiel Mphahlele aims a similar reproach at negritude: 'The poetry of *negritude*, as I see it, is but a repetition of the romantic revival in 19th century Europe...The result of this is that such poetry tells only half of the truth about Africa: its innocence, peace, primitive purity, and never about its violence... its restlessness, its painful paradoxes, its heartbreaks.' E. Mphahlele, 'Replying'

2 Fanon, *The Wretched*, pp. 187–188.

attached to the 'African personality' in the ideology of negritude. 'In Africa, the movement of men of culture is a movement towards the Negro-African culture or the Arab-Moslem culture. It is not specifically towards a national culture. Culture is becoming more and more cut-off from the events of today.'[1] In actual fact a national culture in the countries of the Third World can develop only in connection with a revolutionary re-creation of the economic and social structures, i.e., by a general liberation struggle. Both form and content of a culture, whether in literature, handicrafts or music, are revolutionized by the liberation struggle and differ widely from traditional art. Fanon mentions interesting observations concerning the cultural manifestations of the colonized during the liberation struggle without, unfortunately, going into much detail. There is in the first instance a change in literary themes; they no longer point accusingly at the colonizer but are directly addressed to the colonized. Where handicrafts are concerned, stereotyped forms of expression gradually take on a new dynamism. In ceramics new colours are discovered. Dances and songs display a hardly concealed impatience. One factor all these modifications have in common is their rejection of formalism. The Algerian storytellers revolutionize both the substance of their stories and their manner of presentation. From 1955 onwards the colonial regime proceeded to arrest them systematically. The art specialists coming from the so-called motherland protest in the name of a codified style and suddenly cast themselves in the role of defenders of an authentic native style, which they alone claim to be able to define.[2] 'The struggle for freedom does not give back to the national culture its former value and

[1] ibid., p. 175.
[2] ibid., pp. 193–195.

shapes; this struggle which aims at a fundamentally different set of relations between men cannot leave intact either the form or the content of the people's culture.'[1]

---

[1] ibid., p. 197.

6. Emancipation through Violence

(A) PHILOSOPHICAL AND SOCIOPSYCHOLOGICAL ASPECTS

In our description of the colonial situation we have already pointed out that it was through violence that the colonial powers forced new structures on to the subjected countries. The contacts between the imperialist industrial powers and the agrarian countries of Asia, Africa and Latin America were established and consolidated by soldiers; those countries were conquered and slowly occupied by the army moving from the coast further inland. Subsequently vast areas were handed over to joint-stock companies in order to keep the costs of the colonial administration as low as possible. The natives were forced to work for the conqueror by means of a head-tax which had to be paid in kind. In this way compulsory taxation could initially serve as a substitute for productive investments. The traditional village and tribal economy—basically a subsistence economy—was seriously impaired by the heavy demands made on its labour force, its food production decreased, and the native population was decimated by wars and deteriorating living conditions. Traditional institutions disintegrated or were destroyed by the foreign intrusion. The catastrophic consequences of ruinous exploitation by the joint-stock companies during the phase of conquest could not guarantee a sustained exploitation of the colonies, and after creating an infrastructure geared to an export economy, one therefore proceeded to take the land away from the natives in the fertile areas rich in mineral resources in order to make it available to European entrepreneurs and settlers. Eventually the typical colonial relationships were established on the basis of a systematic exploitation of the natives in mines and plantations. They involved the sale of colonial products at minimal prices in conformity with the demands of the world market, as against the import of finished goods from the metropolitan country at excessive prices.

Historically speaking, we can distinguish certain qualitatively different political practices of colonization since the period of mercantilism; they always corresponded to the level of socioeconomic development of the colonizing country concerned.[1] The period of mercantilism entailed a policy of government-sponsored pillage whilst industrialization and the increasing need for raw materials during the phase of competitive capitalism brought about a more rational organization and a systematic approach to colonial exploitation. Finally, the colonial policy of monopoly capitalism is characterized by the export of capital on the one hand and the increasingly political nature of economic relations between the metropolitan countries and their poverty-stricken dependencies on the other.

Any restructuring of traditional forms of economic organization with a view to the metropolitan country's needs was only possible with the assistance of the army and the brutal force it was capable of applying. The army had to provide for its own maintenance in the colony while at the same time protecting the interests of entrepreneurs and settlers. The violence by which the colonial structures were imposed now became an integral part of the new system. Not only did it show its imprint on the institutional framework but it also

---

[1] See Conrad Schuhler, *Zur politischen Ökonomie der armen Welt* (Munich: Tricent, 1968), especially chapter 4 B.

entered human relations. Both the antagonistic relationship between the colonized and the colonial master and the interpersonal behaviour patterns among the colonized are characterized by violence. The dehumanizing influence of the colonial structures affects all individuals living within the system. 'In other words, for the son of the colonizer violence is inherent in the situation itself, it is the social force that produces him; the son of the colonizer and the son of the Moslem are to the same extent children of the objective violence by which the system is defined . . .'[1] The colonizer bases his violence ideologically on the, initially, passive resistance of the colonized, which is a consequence of the former's violence and serves in turn as its justification. Racism and its practical manifestations—the escalating brutality of oppression—are meant to obviate the counter-violence of the colonized. Its brutality notwithstanding, institutionalized violence retains its economically rational character. In marked contrast to the early phase of colonization, when the settler's violence ruled arbitrarily and unchecked, its function in the organized colonial economy is to assure the exploitation of the natives. However, in the same measure as institutionalized violence guarantees a maximum of economic profit to the colonizer, it reproduces itself among the exploited natives. Oppression and brutality finally reach a point where there is only one way out left for the colonized person: to the violence of the colonizer he opposes his own violence aiming at liberation:[2]

---

[1] J. P. Sartre, *Critique de la raison dialectique* (Paris: Gallimard 1960), p. 675

[2] The extent to which the outbreak of violence can be ascribed to physical misery on the one hand, or to the development of consciousness and the corresponding political organization on the other, differs from country to country and depends on the existing economic structure, i.e., the importance of the modern, mechanized sector of the economy and the tenurial relationships of peasants to the land. In Fanon's theory the misery of the rural masses is the decisive factor for the outbreak of violence.

> ... I believe that for oppressed and subdued minorities there is a right of resistance based on "natural law", a right to use extra-legal means as soon as the legal ones have proved inadequate. Law and order are always and everywhere the law and order of those who protect the established hierarchy ... There is no judge above them except the established authorities, the police, and their own conscience. By using violence, they do not initiate any new chain of violent acts but merely break the existing one.[1]

Marcuse here points to an aspect of revolutionary violence which is essential for an understanding of Fanon's theory; the violence of the colonized is an act of emancipation, it is in all instances nothing but his answer to the acts of coercion perpetrated against him; as counter-violence it aims in principle at removing the existing authority relationship based on force and superseding the factors conducive to alienation. 'On the other hand political theory and practice are aware of historical situations in which violence is the necessary and essential element of progress...If undertaken in the interest of the whole against particular interests of oppression, terror can become a necessity and an obligation.'[2] Through the act of violence the colonized is capable of freeing himself from his reified status and becoming once more a human being; 'Decolonization is always a violent phenomenon...Decolonization is the veritable creation of new men...the "thing" which has been colonized becomes man during the same process by which it frees itself'.[3]

---

[1] Herbert Marcuse, *Kritik der reinen Toleranz* (Frankfurt: Suhrkamp, 1966), p. 127.

[2] Herbert Marcuse, *Kultur und Gesellschaft 2* (Frankfurt: Suhrkamp, 1965), p. 134.

[3] Frantz Fanon, *The Wretched of the Earth*, trans. C. Farrington (London: MacGibbon & Kee, 1965), pp. 29–30.

Theoretically Fanon's concept of violence is unadmittedly derived from Hegel via Sartre's philosophy.[1] Colonial domination and colonial servitude are a new historical manifestation of the master-bondsman relationship analysed by Hegel. According to Hegel, the bondsman can become free by objectifying himself in his work; he spares no pains working against his own negativity and through this very fact achieves liberation. Hegel never failed to emphasize this unheroic element in the bourgeoisie. The master is reduced to dependence, he loses his freedom by relating to things only through the bondsman. He merely functions as the controller of certain processes which must lead to recognition, whereas the bondsman mediates this recognition by his conflict with external nature and thus constitutes himself as the bourgeois individual. This process of recognition is based on a manifest power relationship. According to Fanon, the possibility of gaining recognition through the bourgeois working process conceived as emancipation is not open to the colonial bondsman. He lives in a world of overt, unveiled inequality where integration and cohesion are solely guaranteed by force. In Fanon's view the colonial bondsman also asserts his true self through work but his own conception of work differs from Hegel's: 'For the native this violence represents the absolute line of action. The militant is also a man who works'.[2] Thus understood work means the use of active violence; for the colonized, 'to work means to work for the death of the settler'.[3] By simply identifying the spontaneous act of violence with work, Fanon leaves that element

---

[1] Sartre, who analyses violence under the aspect of deficiency, starts from the premise that violence always manifests itself as counter-violence. The violence of the colonized who rebels against the colonial system is always derivative; it is the violence of the colonizer which is now directed against himself: 'The violence of the rebel is the violence of the *colon*, there is none other'. Sartre, *Critique*, p. 687.

[2] Fanon, *The Wretched*, p. 66.

[3] Ibid., p. 67.

out of consideration which in Hegel's theory allows the emancipation of the serf; the material working process, the chance of objectification through work is neglected in favour of the psychological emancipation process through violence. Although Hegel does not fail to see the possibility of man asserting himself by fighting against his like, he rejects this possibility as not bringing a permanent solution. His attitude toward revolution is ambivalent. On the one hand revolutions are the principle of world history, which presides over the necessary destruction of institutions drained of substance. 'Thus the revolution and the philosophy paving its way are, it is true, "destructive", but what they destroy was already destroyed in itself: the horrible state of society, misery, vileness, "incredible shamelessness and unlawfulness, the total absence of rights for the individual in the legal and political spheres, in thought and conscience".'[1] Revolution is thus an expression of emancipatory self-determination. On the other hand, any experience of the revolution entails terror:

> Universal freedom can thus produce neither a positive achievement nor a deed; there is left for it only negative action; it is merely the rage and fury of destruction . . . The sole and only work and deed accomplished by universal freedom is therefore *death* . . . the most cold-blooded and meaningless death of all, with no more significance than the cleaving of a head of cabbage or swallowing a draught of water . . . All these determinate elements disappear with the disaster and ruin that overtake the self in the state of absolute freedom; its negation is meaningless death, sheer horror of the negative which has nothing positive in it, nothing that gives a filling.[2]

---

[1] Joachim Ritter, *Hegel und die französische Revolution* (Frankfurt: Suhrkamp, 1965), p. 22.

[2] G. W. F. Hegel, *The Phenomenology of Mind* (London: G. Allen & Unwin Ltd, 1931), pp. 604–608.

Terror has no progressive function but is a relapse into abstract subjectivism. Revolutionary violence is an expression of impotence in the face of historical development: abstract subjectivity tries to stand up against the course of the world. Revolutionary violence is identical with absolute liberty and terror. This ambivalence in Hegel's attitude toward revolution has two reasons. The revolution concreticizes the problems of how to achieve a lasting realization of liberty without, however, solving it. According to Hegel, the negativity of revolution consists of the fact that it has hitherto not found and realized any lasting political solutions. In addition, terror and violence, being anarchic elements, are an expression of mere subjectivity. While Hegel, who views revolutionary processes only in terms of objective events, rejects violence as a line of action authorized by the subjective consciousness, Fanon's analysis emphasizes this very same conscious action on the part of the revolutionaries. In interpreting the role of violence in the process of decolonization, Fanon stresses the subjective side. The awakening revolutionary consciousness motivated by the use of violence is at the same time cause and consequence of the anti-colonial liberation struggle: 'The colonised man finds his freedom in and through violence. This rule of conduct enlightens the agent because it indicates to him the means and the end'.[1]

Fanon conceives of violence as a process in which two phases can be distinguished. In the first phase violence is directed spontaneously, without organization and as yet without any political concept against the foreign intruder, the colonial master. In the second phase, which extends into the period of formal independence, it gets organized and dovetails into the socialist revolution. While during the first phase violence tends to do away with the psychological torpor and alienation

[1] Fanon, *The Wretched*, p. 67.

of the colonized, during the second phase it changes the capitalist colonial structures which produce such alienated behaviour. In accordance with the sociopsychological approach in all of his works Fanon devotes his attention mainly to the first phase of violence.

The colonial world is a bipartite world in which colonizer and colonized face each other without any chance of reconciliation. There is no possibility of a compromise. The colonized knows that his desperate situation allows of only one solution: taking the colonizer's place by violent means. Wherever the colonized comes into contact with the world of his master, the latter demonstrates his strength and superiority to him. The borderline between the world of the colonizer and that of the colonized is marked by army cordons and police-posts. 'The native is always on the alert, for since he can only make out with difficulty the many symbols of the colonial world, he is never sure whether or not he has crossed the frontier. Confronted with a world ruled by the settler, the native is always presumed guilty.'[1] Despite his apparent torpor the colonized is, however, never truly domesticated: 'The native's muscles are always tensed'.[2]

Initially his pent-up aggressiveness is released in actions which as yet do not affect the true cause of all aggressions, the colonial regime and its representatives. These actions can, however, only serve as a temporary compensation; they are themselves an expression of the alienation which still prevents the colonized from safeguarding his own interests. Finally, however, the spontaneous outbreak of violence occurs, and it is often touched off by some minor provocation. A precondition for the beginning of the active phase of the liberation struggle is, firstly, that the given historical situation

---

[1] ibid., p. 42.
[2] ibid., p. 42.

makes the enforcement of emancipatory violence possible and, secondly, that the subjective propagation of this objective situation through international revolutionary communication processes (e.g., the anti-colonial liberation struggle of one people has an exemplary character for all colonized) is guaranteed. Now all of a sudden the colonized masses grasp intuitively, according to Fanon, that their liberation can only be achieved through violence. At this stage of direct, sanguinary revolt violence lacks as yet a political and strategic orientation; for the time being it has a sociopsychological function, and in this form it is a necessary precondition for the organized liberation struggle. The alienation of the colonized is above all evidenced by the fact that the scale of values set up by the colonizer is accepted by the oppressed themselves. Due to his superior strength the colonizer actually appears to the colonized as the superman which racism intends him to represent. By killing his oppressor, by chasing him away through violence the colonized cures himself of colonial neurosis and thus achieves his freedom of action which seemed to have been lost in apathy and torpor. 'For in the first days of the revolt you must kill: to shoot down a European is to kill two birds with one stone, to destroy an oppressor and the man he oppresses at the same time: there remain a dead man, and a free man.'[1] The colonized man, 'deciding to embody history in his own person',[2] frees himself from his inferiority complex by violence, breaks away from his contemplative attitude, sheds his anxiety and rehabilitates himself in his own eyes. 'For the native life can only spring up again from the rotting corpse of the settler.'[3]

---

[1] Sartre, Preface to *The Wretched*, pp. 18–19.

[2] Fanon, *The Wretched*, p. 33.

[3] ibid., p. 72. In this connection one could argue: If the relationship between the colonized and the colonizer is considered in psychoanalytical categories in analogy to the father-son relationship, the outbreak of spontaneous violence

[*Notes continued on the next page*]

Apart from the liberating psychological effect, violence has an integrating function, both politically and with regard to the dynamics of the group. Only by performing an irrevocable action, an act of violence, does the individual qualify for a political activity in the resistance movement. It is true that such action may only take place symbolically and thus virtually check violence rather than unleash it; in the Mau-Mau movement oath-taking was substituted for violence and thus led to a control of the Kikuyu, contrary to the current opinion. Admission to the terrorist groups of the Algerian Liberation Front, on the other hand, could only be gained after an assassination attempt. Through this act of violence the return into the colonial system is barred; thus violence appears as the ideal means of reintegration: 'This assumed responsibility for violence allows both strayed and outlawed members of the group to come back again and to find their place once more, to become integrated. Violence is thus seen as comparable to a royal pardon'.[1] At the same time, however, this insistence on an irrevocable, compromising act points to the unpolitical character of spontaneous outbursts of violence and expresses

could be interpreted as patricide. The facts in favour of this argument are that the colonizer, like the father, is in possession of all means of subsistence and denies them to the colonized, to which the latter reacts with envy and the spontaneous desire to take the colonizer's, i.e., the father's, place. According to Freud the consequence of patricide is the enthronement of the 'bad conscience' which, if we carry the analogy further, would be a source of new complexes in the colonized. The effect of this sense of guilt is that the sons adopt the father's norms, thus guaranteeing their continued existence. A first objection to this analogy is that a libidinous bond is a constituent element in the father-son relationship, which has no parallel in colonialism. To what extent the murder of the colonizer gives rise to new psychic complexes of social relevance is, however, a moot point. In psychoanalytical theory the murder of his father cannot be an act of liberation for the son. On the other hand the colonial revolution, inaugurated by the violent exorcism of the colonial master, undoubtedly is an act of liberation. In any discussion of this nature Fanon's own objections to the use of psychoanalytical categories for the analysis of politico-economic phenomena ought to be taken into account.

[1] Fanon, *The Wretched*, p. 67.

certain doubts on the part of revolutionary leaders as to the uncompromising attitude of the oppressed towards the colonial system.

Fanon clearly sees that the spontaneous outburst of violence, however necessary it might be as a psychological preparation of the colonized for the liberation struggle, must be very quickly organized and politicized if it is not to be nipped in the bud like so many sporadic revolts against colonialism. 'You can hold out for three days—maybe even for three months—on the strength of the admixture of sheer resentment contained in the mass of the people; but you won't win a national war, you'll never overthrow the terrible enemy machine, and you won't change human beings if you forget to raise the standard of consciousness of the rank and file.'[1]

If the uprising is to graduate into a revolution, the racially motivated hatred against the colonizer of the initial period must be differentiated by political indoctrination and divested of its racial component. During the second phase of the struggle it is of crucial importance that the undifferentiated nationalist consciousness of the insurgents evolves towards political and economic awareness. Henceforth 'the settler is not simply the man that must be killed'.[2] The people must give up the primitive manicheism taken over wholesale from the colonial master; it must learn that there are Europeans who take an active part in the liberation struggle, and that on the other hand 'you get Blacks who are whiter than the Whites'.[3] Thus in the course of their struggle the consciousness of the oppressed attains to limited, inconstant truths which can be modified by new events any time.

---

[1] ibid., p. 108.
[2] ibid., p. 116.
[3] ibid., p. 115.

The decisive result of this process is that the colonized lays the foundations of the new reality through his own actions; he achieves a self-confident attitude toward his own history and, according to Fanon, turns from being the object of the course of history to being its subject through the liberating act of violence. A people which has thus achieved an active attitude towards its own history, can no longer be mislead by any sham reforms or manoeuvres of the colonial power:

> Violence alone, violence committed by the people, violence organized and educated by its leaders, makes it possible for the masses to understand social truths and gives the key to them. Without that struggle, without that knowledge of the practice of action, there's nothing but a fancy-dress parade and the blare of trumpets. There's nothing save a minimum of readaptation, a few reforms at the top, a flag waving: and down there at the bottom an undivided mass, still living in the middle ages, endlessly marking time.[1]

The enlightening and emancipatory tendency of Fanon's theory of violence and its special historical relevance for the anticolonial liberation struggle becomes evident when it is set off against Sorel on the one hand and Engels on the other. While Sorel hypostatizes the psychological elements and shapes them into a myth, Engels in his own analysis dispenses with them altogether: 'Power in this day and age means the army and the fleet'.[2] The model which determines Engels' orientation is the relationship between Robinson and Friday, in which the technical equipment of the individual immediately defines his potential political dominance. But only if the power potential of the impoverished masses in the colonies is compared with the modern military machine of the oppressor in an abstract fashion does violence on the part of the colonized appear a

---

[1] ibid., p. 117.

[2] Friedrich Engels, *Anti-Dühring*, in K. Marx and F. Engels, *Werke*, vol. 20 (Berlin: Dietz, 1962), p. 154.

counsel of despair. In the Third World, where technological strength is inferior to the military potential of the industrial power, the organizational problems of violence take on a central significance. There is no other way of constituting counter-violence. Fanon criticizes Engels for overlooking the fact that the counter-violence of the colonized is something qualitatively new and he points out that 'the native's guerilla warfare would be of no value as opposed to other means of violence if it did not form a new element in the world-wide process of competition between trusts and monopolies'.[1] He reproaches Engels with anticipating in his theory of violence the kind of reformism which rationalizes its inertia by pointing to the enemy's superior military technology.

At a cursory glance Sorel's theory of violence is much closer to Fanon's approach. Sorel and Fanon have in common that they conceive of the struggle of the poor against the rich only in terms of violence; both of them tackle the interiorization of oppression by the poor: 'What is truly essential here is to give the poor an absolute confidence in their strength; in order to achieve this result one must overcome the traditions of subservience with which they have been indoctrinated from their youth'.[2] However, while Fanon, whose stance is determined by humanist considerations and the desire to enlighten, is averse to any myth and analyses conditions scientifically, myth occupies a central position in Sorel's thought. These differences can be derived from their divergent conceptions of violence. For Sorel violence is a natural, instinctive

---

[1] Fanon, *The Wretched*, p. 51. 'Revolutionary theory becomes an invincible power the moment it has seized the masses. In a revolutionary war the political superiority of the people will be transformed into material violence'. see Nguyen Giap, quoted by Steinhaus, *Vietnam* (Frankfurt a.M.: Verlag neue Kritik, 1967). p. 41.

[2] Georges Sorel, quoted by Hans Barth, *Masse und Mythos* (Hamburg: Rowohlt, 1959), p. 111.

constant in human nature, whose eruption must not be thwarted. A 'tendency towards violence' is inherent in man. 'Sorel's defence of violence on this side of good and evil remained isolated from the revolutionary reality of his age; whatever influence he might have had was on the side of the counter-revolution.'[1] Fanon, on the other hand, analyses violence in its historical and economic context as a phenomenon derived from, and brought about by, the process of colonial exploitation. His concept of violence is not restricted to the moment of its spontaneous outburst but is differentiated in social terms and interpreted in the context of a revolutionary upheaval of the social structure.

(B) A CONCRETE EXAMPLE: THE ALGERIAN REVOLUTION

The central idea for any understanding of Fanon's theory of violence is that of a total psychic transformation of man through the *praxis* of violence in the liberation struggle. In analysing the Algerian Revolution, Fanon tries to prove by giving the example of individual social phenomena to what extent the liberation struggle modifies both the social structures and the individuals themselves.[2] The decisive factor in creating a 'nouvelle humanité', as Fanon calls it, is the process by which in the course of the struggle the mechanisms of concealment obscuring the inner workings of the colonial society become increasingly transparent to the individual and lose their hold on him. The revolutionary practice solves those conflicts and disposes of the psychological obstacles which have been described as phenomena of social and intellectual alienation. By way of an example we wish to discuss Fanon's study of the Algerian

---

1 Marcuse, *Kultur und Gesellschaft 2*, p. 139.

2 See F. Fanon, *L'an V de la Revolution Algérienne* (Paris: Maspero 1959); English translation, *Studies in a Dying Colonialism*, intr. Adolfo Gilly, trans. Haakon Chevalier (New York: Monthly Review Press, 1965).

Revolution entitled *Algeria Unveiled.*[1] The other studies, which investigate the same revolutionary restructuring of various social institutions, deal with the transformation of the traditional Algerian family structure and the social functions of radio and medicine, which undergo modifications during the struggle.

During the colonial period the fight against the veil was in the foreground of the colonial propaganda campaign for the 'emancipation of the Algerian woman'. Fanon interprets this endeavour as an attempt at deforming Algerian culture and destroying the potential of resistance drawing on it: 'The officials of the French administration in Algeria committed to destroying the people's originality, and under instructions to bring about the disintegration, at whatever cost, of forms of existence likely to evoke a national reality directly or indirectly, were to concentrate their efforts at the wearing of the veil'.[2] But the perseverance of the colonized in defending certain traditions expresses their refusal to part with the remains of a national existence. Any abandonment would spell collusion with the colonizer; for the colonized it would be a further step on the path to total subjection: 'Every veil that fell...was a negative expression of the fact that Algeria was beginning to deny herself and was accepting the rape of the colonizer'.[3] The colonized opposes a cult of the veil to the colonizer's persistent struggle to abolish it. It is only in the face of the colonizer's propaganda that the colonized takes a staunch stand in favour of a formerly insignificant element of his culture. Fanon interprets this comportment as a psychological law of colonization: 'In an initial phase, it is the action, the plan of the occupier that determine the centres of resistance around which a people's will

[1] ibid., p. 35–63.
[2] ibid., p. 37.
[3] ibid., p. 42.

to survive becomes organized. It is the white man who creates the Negro. But it is the Negro who creates negritude. To the colonialist offensive against the veil, the colonized opposes the cult of the veil'.[1] By adducing examples of similar mechanisms Fanon proves that there is no sense in speaking of 'counter-acculturation' in a colonial situation, while the actual attitude involved is one of 'counter-assimilation', the maintenance of a cultural and thus national peculiarity. Fanon illustrates his interpretation of colonial emancipation propaganda with the accounts of dreams of European patients. From these dreams it can be gathered that the European's attitude to the Algerian woman is a reflection of his relationship to colonized society. 'Whenever, in dreams having an erotic content, a European meets an Algerian woman, the specific features of his relations with the colonized society manifest themselves.'[2] Even in healthy Europeans the dreams are of an extraordinary brutality; in their dreams, the Algerian woman does not appear as an individual, identifiable person but always in numbers. In the relationship of the European male to the Algerian female we find a mixture of aggressiveness and frustration. This aggressiveness is as a norm expressed by the wish to unveil and rape her; the frustration is brought about by the fact that although she can see him, he can never see her. The attitude of the Algerian male toward the veil, on the other hand, is traditionally unambiguous. He does not make any effort to guess the veiled face but endeavours on the contrary to ignore the women altogether. Within the traditional framework this behaviour itself can only be interpreted as an expression of social repression, while the processes set in motion by the liberation struggle give it a new dimension: traditional behaviour geared to political aims becomes functional.

---

[1] ibid., p. 47.
[2] ibid., pp. 45–46.

During the liberation struggle the veil suddenly takes on a new significance. The Algerians' attitude towards it undergoes a fundamental change, which can only be understood as a reaction to political changes. Starting from 1955 the form of the struggle, especially in the cities, requires the active participation of women. The insistence on retaining the veil —formerly a latent expression of resistance against the occupying forces—now becomes a handicap. The withdrawn, 'veiled' life of the Algerian woman initially renders her revolutionary action difficult. During the first phase of her active participation she still retains the veil, but when the scene of the struggle shifts to the European areas of the city, she suddenly takes it off. In compliance with tactical requirements she changes from European dress to the veil and back again several times in the course of the war, depending on whether she has to operate unobtrusively in European quarters or to carry weapons or other materials hidden under her traditional costume. Only an analysis of the psychological significance of the veil for the woman wearing it can throw light on the political importance that can be attributed to such changes. In traditional society the whole body of the young Algerian female is wrapped up in the veil that protects and isolates her. Fanon quotes from the accounts and dreams of unveiled women which are evidence of the traumatic effect of sudden unveiling: the body seems to break into pieces, the limbs stretch to infinity, an intense feeling of imperfection, even of nakedness, is experienced. The normal sense of orientation gets totally deranged, the woman is unable to estimate distances with any degree of certainty, she suffers from disturbances of equilibrium. Nonetheless the Algerian woman quickly adapts herself to her new role; her insecurity but also her moral scruples vanish in the face of the demands made on her in the struggle for liberty. Very similar processes can be observed in the course of the transformation of traditional family structures. The family accepts the sudden emancipation of the Algerian woman, occasioned by her revolutionary activity side-by-side with men, without any marked resistance. In like manner the father's traditional position of authority *vis-à-vis* his son, and the son's precedence over his sister are reduced in favour of a new authority: the common revolutionary aim.

The transformation of the tradition-directed norms of behaviour described above gives the lie to the colonialist view which considers the continued wearing of the veil as the mere expression of a religious, magical or fanatical attitude. When in 1958 French colonialism again launched a massive campaign of Europeanization, the Algerian women spontaneously resumed the wearing of the veil. To counter this new offensive they fell back on their old reactions. But at this juncture the veil had definitely lost its purely traditional dimension; it had become an instrument geared to a political purpose. This functional change was indicative of far-reaching social and psychological changes in Algerian society: 'Removed and reassumed again and again, the veil has been manipulated, transformed into a technique of camouflage, into a means of struggle. The virtually taboo character assumed by the veil in the colonial situation disappeared almost entirely in the course of the liberating struggle'.[1]

Fanon's description of the way in which traditional structures and institutions were transformed in the course of the fight for freedom is undoubtedly correct. The question remains, however, whether the transformations observed have been institutionalized and developed further in a revolutionary context. The present situation in Algeria does not seem to indicate any such development. Both the traditional family

[1] ibid., p. 61.

structures and the social position of women have not been modified within the framework of a new social order such as Fanon saw it emerge during the revolution. In the final analysis the reasons for his misjudgement can be attributed to his conception of violence. The changes which could be observed during the war of liberation were brought about under duress; they were motivated by political developments which also reverberated in the growth of consciousness. In the economic sector, however, there occurred, and there are to be found up till now, no comparable thoroughgoing changes. As long as unemployment is rampant, as long as universal primary education fails to be introduced and class differences do not only persist but are in actual fact even further exacerbated, while the pronounced differences between town and country remain unaltered, there is no possibility of the traditional structures undergoing any revolutionary changes, although they may have been badly shaken by the violent events of the liberation struggle. In China and Cuba, where the revolution brought about thoroughgoing structural changes, the women actually succeeded in freeing themselves from traditional ties and achieving a status of social equality which does not just remain a matter of form. Violence as such merely furnishes the basis for achieving emancipation; emancipation itself can only be the result of a socioeconomic process which in the main must be defined as a revolutionary working process.

7. Conditions of Emancipation

(A) CONSCIOUSNESS AND POLITICAL PRAXIS

If the emancipatory violence used in the anticolonial liberation struggle is to achieve the revolutionary aim of restructuring existing conditions, certain prerequisites both of a psychological and a political and organizational nature have to be fulfilled. In the long run the success of the revolution depends on whether or not developments of consciousness have been set in motion in the oppressed during the first phase of the revolution. Their indignation must be channelled and conceptualized to such an extent that they gain an insight into the mechanisms of their own oppression. Only such an insight which guides the masses beyond the rashness of their first violent reactions against the oppressor allows spontaneous political initiatives which do not just remain the isolated acts of individuals. The only task that devolves on national leaders in this situation is to channel such spontaneity; they must beware lest they act alone, in lieu of the masses: 'The peasants themselves have erected these statues, and a time will come when they will tear them down with their own hands; there is no need for others to do so prematurely in their place . . . The peasants themselves must destroy the images of the Gods . . . it would be an error to take the peasants' place in this matter'.[1] The importance of making the masses realize

[1] Mao Tse-Tung, *Report of an investigation into the peasant movement in Hunan*, (Peking: Foreign Languages Press, 1953).

the necessity of operating on their own, which is here emphasized by Mao Tse-tung in a report on the peasant movement in Hunan in 1927, should not be underestimated both during the phase of the direct struggle against the colonial power and that of conscious nation-building. Fanon emphasizes the necessity of this process with specific reference to developments taking place after independence has been formally attained: 'Certainly, there may well be need of engineers and architects, sometimes completely foreign engineers and architects; but the local party leaders should be already present, so that the new techniques can make their way into the cerebral desert of the citizen, so that the bridge in whole and in part can be taken up and conceived, and the responsibility for it assumed by the citizen. In this way, and in this way only, everything is possible'.[1]

At first sight Fanon's concepts bear a marked resemblance to the Chinese and Cuban theories of the anti-colonial revolution. But although he generally considers the peasantry the spearhead of the revolution and stresses the importance of implanting a new revolutionary consciousness in the masses, the fact remains that there is a fundamental divergence of views when it comes to analysing the notion of spontaneity and defining the concept of revolutionary violence.

Fanon conceives both spontaneity and violence as political categories divorced from the context of the overall economic process of reproduction. It is true that Fanon realizes the dangers that threaten revolutionary praxis if political spontaneity is allowed to go unchecked. But he remains at the prepolitical stage of enlightenment when he puts too much trust in the effect of awakening consciousness and demands the politization of the masses in the abstract:

---

[1] F. Fanon, *The Wretched of the Earth*, trans. C. Farrington (London: MacGibbon & Kee, 1965), p. 160.

> Now the political education of the masses is seen to be a historic necessity. That spectacular volunteer movement which meant to lead the colonised people to supreme sovereignty at one fell swoop . . . that strength which gave you hope: all now are seen in the light of experience to be symptoms of a very great weakness . . . While (the colonised person) grasped at the mirage of his muscles' own immediacy, he made no real progress along the road to knowledge. His consciousness remained rudimentary.[1]

Revolutionary political praxis, which implies both emancipation through violence and simultaneously emancipation through work as its material concomitant, is one-sidedly interpreted by Fanon as the mere practicing of violence. In Fanon's theory emancipation only means political praxis as revolutionary deed, as an act of violence; emancipation is understood in the first instance as a process of individual psychology in the oppressed mediated by the dynamics of a group. Political praxis is identical with violence aiming at emancipation, and this violence, which remains unrelated to its material correlate—the social working process—is conceived of as a force structuring consciousness. The structure of the colonized's consciousness is Manichean; it is conditioned by the antagonisms of colonial society. The colonized is alienated from himself. The violence of the colonized, in its quality as counter-violence aiming at emancipation, has as its function to structure the identity of each consciousness. It aims at the self-realization of the individual in an objective correlation with the oppressed collective.

Fanon's reduction of violence to the mere act of exercising it in a revolutionary context during the liberation struggle, and his neglect of the politico-economic aspects of the anticolonial revolution result from the fact that he himself being a colonial, his attention is narrowly focussed on the colonies. His refusal to include the metropolitan countries in his

---

[1] ibid., p. 110.

analysis may well be a legitimate expression of his political resentment, but it cannot be justified in the context of his theory. Fanon's political theory is unable to link processes of consciousness with a political line of action. This would only be possible in connection with a politico-economic analysis of socially relevant forces. His category of mediation is violence, conceived mainly in terms of individual and social psychology. Violence conceived in terms of revolutionizing social work is disregarded in his analysis.

Spontaneity and violence are identical in Fanon's theory. The problem of institutionalizing spontaneity and assigning it a function in the process of altering the economic structures is not tackled. The fact that Fanon did not live to see the phase of reconstruction after the victory over French colonialism is insufficient to account for his omission of this aspect of the problem. His theoretical starting point which reduces spontaneity to the mere act of revolutionary violence precludes any further reflections which would give the function of spontaneity in revolutionary working processes its due weight. The differences with the Chinese and Cuban theory clearly emerge: 'From an ideological viewpoint, our fundamental task is to find the formula which will perpetuate in daily life these heroic attitudes (of total commitment to the revolutionary cause)', writes Che Guevara.[1] In Cuba an attempt is made by means of mobilization and industrialization campaigns to give revolutionary commitment a more enduring form. The new man is as much a product of the changed economic mode of production as an expression of revolutionized consciousness: 'In this period of the construction of socialism, we can see the new man being born. His image is as yet unfinished;

---

[1] Ernesto Che Guevara, 'Socialism and Man in Cuba', (1965), in *Che, Selected Works of Ernesto Guevara* (Cambridge, Mass., and London: MIT Press, 1969), p. 156.

in fact, it will never be finished, for the process advances parallel to the development of new economic forms ... This is why it is so important to choose correctly the instrument for the mobilization of the masses'.[1]

While for Fanon spontaneity is a potentially revolutionary but substantially pre-conscious, immediate reaction, in the Cuban and Chinese conception it has its decidedly rational aspects. The revolutionary avant-garde who has reached a higher level of consciousness assures the perpetuation of spontaneous revolutionary actions; not only does it channel spontaneous eruptions of violence but it also emits activating impulses touching off political upheavals that lead to radical changes in the existing structures. In Fanon's theory there is no room for any avant-garde. The members of nationalist parties fleeing from colonialist repression to the countryside encounter the latently revolutionary peasant masses and merely put their technical know-how at their disposal:

> These men get used to talking to the peasants. They discover that the mass of the country people have never ceased to think of the problem of their liberation except in terms of violence, in terms of taking back the land from the foreigners, in terms of national struggle, and of armed insurrection ... The men coming from the towns learn their lessons in the hard school of the people; and at the same time these men open classes for the people in military and political education ... The armed struggle has begun.[2]

In the resistance potential of the peasantry Fanon discovers an inherent rationality not subjected to any organized political control and whose political criteria

---

[1] ibid., pp. 159–160.

[2] Fanon, *The Wretched*, pp. 101–102. In his investigation of the guerilla struggle in Latin America Régis Debray arrives at a similar analysis: 'Here the small initial groups from the cities have their first daily contact with rural realities, little by little adjust themselves to their demands, and begin to understand from the inside the aspirations of their people; they cast aside political verbosity and make of these aspirations their programme of action'. Régis Debray, *Revolution in the Revolution? Armed and Political Struggle in Latin America* (New York and London: MR Press, 1967), p. 112.

he fails to elucidate altogether. Still, this ill-defined political consciousness is said to assure an undogmatic development commensurate with the specific requirements of the Third World. Mao Tse-tung likewise discerns the revolutionary potential in the exploited peasant masses: 'The main force in the hard and bitter struggle taking place in the countryside has always been the impoverished peasants . . . The general direction given to the revolution by these peasants has always been the correct one'.[1] However, without the groundwork of political orientation and organization carried out by the Marxist cadres the revolution would have bogged down in revolt, and revolutionary protest would have been nipped in the bud by reactionary reforms: 'Frantz Fanon's description . . . does not make allowances for the actual situation in the Chinese countryside in 1927. The Marxist militants brought a new motive force, a means, even if it had not yet reached maturation, of solving the problems which the Chinese peasants had been unable to solve in the course of the numerous class revolts that pervade the history of China . . .'[2]

Fanon's analysis of the class structure in the Third World countries, which hypostatizes a single phase of the liberation struggle—the eruption of spontaneous violence—without any attempt at differentiation, does not do justice to the actual conditions and their revolutionary implications in those countries. His erroneous interpretation of the Algerian Revolution as a socialist one is significant in this respect. Lenin in 1901 polemicized against pre-industrial theories of spontaneity which, according to him, strictly speaking only helped to perpetuate existing historical conditions; his statement may well apply to Fanon's theory of

1 Mao Tse-Tung, *Report*.
2 Enrica Collotti-Pischel, *La Révolution ininterrompue*, trans. A. Marchand (Paris: TM, Julliard 1964), p. 139.

spontaneous violence: 'This shows . . . that *all* worship of the spontaneity of the working-class movement, all belittling of the "conscious element"...means...*a strengthening of the influence of bourgeois ideology upon the workers* . . . There is much talk about spontaneity. But the *spontaneous* development of the working-class movement leads to its subordination to bourgeois ideology . . .'[1]

(B) SOCIAL AND ECONOMIC PRE-CONDITIONS

Fanon distinguishes three social classes in the colonies: the peasantry which constitutes the mass of the population, the proletariat which is still at its embryonic stage and numerically insignificant, and the national bourgeoisie. With certain reservations he considers the *lumpenproletariat* as the fourth estate, since this group may possibly gain some significance in the process of decolonization: 'For the *lumpenproletariat*, that horde of starving men, uprooted from their tribe and from their clan, constitutes one of the most spontaneous and the most radically revolutionary forces of a colonised people'.[2] It vegetates in the slums on the outskirts of the cities and is responsive to revolutionary agitation in consequence of its social misery and disintegration. On the other hand, it becomes for the very same reason an easy prey for colonial propaganda. In Algeria, the 'harkis', or native professional soldiers in the colonial army, were preponderantly recruited from among the *lumpenproletariat*.

By comparison the social and political situation of the proletariat is unequivocal; it is most strongly integrated into the capitalist process of production based on the division of labour and doubtless belongs to the privileged part of colonial society. It is necessary

1 W. I. Lenin, 'What is to be done?' in Lenin, *Selected Works*, in three volumes (Moscow: Foreign Languages Publishing House, 1960), vol. 1, pp. 155–157 (Author's italics).

2 Fanon, *The Wretched*, p. 103.

and irreplaceable for the proper functioning of the colonial machinery of domination: 'It is these elements which constitute the most faithful elements of the nationalist parties, and who because of the privileged place which they hold in the colonial system constitute also the "bourgeois" fraction of the colonized people . . . It is these classes that will struggle against obscurantist traditions, that will change old customs, and that will thus enter into open conflict with the old granite block upon which the nation rests.'[1] While the urban proletariat is materially and ideologically corrupted by the close contact with the colonial power and attempts to come to terms with colonialism on the basis of group interest, the peasants have always evaded integration into the colonial system. The social structure of the peasantry has preserved its traditional and corporate character: 'From all eternity . . . the country people had more or less kept their individuality free from colonial impositions . . . The peasant's pride, his hesitation to go down into the towns and to mingle with the world that the foreigner had built, his perpetual shrinking back at the approach of the agents of colonial administration: all these reactions signified that to the dual world of the settler he opposed his own duality'.[2] The level of consciousness with regard to an integration into the colonial society here becomes by implication the distinguishing mark of class membership and revolutionary potential. Since the peasants are less alienated, and their inarticulate resistance is not weakened by any compromise, they are the agents o^ violence and the subjects of revolutionary change: 'And it is clear that in the colonial countries the peasants alone are revolutionary, for they have nothing to lose and everything to gain. The starving peasant, outside the class system, is the first

---

1 ibid., p. 88.
2 ibid., pp. 110–111.

among the exploited to discover that only violence pays. For him there is no compromise, no possible coming to terms'.[1]

Here it becomes again obvious that Fanon's categories are derived from social psychology; although they are adequate to describe the psychological phenomena of alienation, they become irrelevant when it is a question of assessing the class structure, in other words, the relationships of economic dependence. An exclusive recourse to phenomena of consciousness renders any differentiations which would result from a precise analysis of the individual's position in the production process superfluous. The role Fanon assigns to the national bourgeoisie in a crude schematic outline of neocolonial conditions is of an unequivocally counter-revolutionary nature. In his analysis he fails to make a distinction between comprador and national bourgeoisie, merchant and administrative bourgeoisie as well as between their various social and political functions.

Fanon gives us a phenomenological description of neocolonialism which is in general correct but which is restricted to the conditions in the former colonies. It does not include any analysis of international relationships of dependence nor of the background and motives of modern imperialist policy. His interest is focussed on four main points: the function of the native middle class, the role of the national leader, the position of the party, and the organization of the army.

The national bourgeoisie in underdeveloped countries is numerically weak and without accumulated capital. It refuses to follow the path of revolution. After independence it takes over the positions abandoned by the former masters without changing the economic structure of colonialism. No effort is made to

---

[1] ibid., p. 48.

set up a local industry or, in the case of an economy based on monoculture, to diversify the cultivation of crops, but unprocessed raw materials are exported as in the past. Members of the national bourgeoisie mainly derive their profits from their activity as middlemen between the former mother-country and the now independent colony, as well as from taxes. 'To them, nationalization quite simply means the transfer into native hands of those unfair advantages which are a legacy of the colonial period.'[1] In contrast to the European bourgeoisie which exercised a progressive function during the early stages of industrialization, the 'bourgeoisie' in the developing countries is parasitical and redundant. Fanon's concept of the bourgeoisie embraces both merchant and administrative bourgeoisie. The parasitical character of the latter objectively results from the fact that at independence the colony takes over from the colonial power an administrative machinery out of all proportion to the actual administrative needs of the country and fulfilling mainly ceremonial functions which draw their inspiration from the example of the colonial power. This unproductive and to a large extent redundant administrative bourgeoisie draws its considerable income from internal revenue, which is thus withheld from useful investment, while the merchant bourgeoisie lives on import-export business which serves to perpetuate or even further aggravate the existing international division of labour between the suppliers of raw materials and the industrial nations. Their profits are either invested unproductively in prestige projects, consumed, or transferred to foreign banks.[2] The middle class tries to interrupt the incipient process of emancipation by force in order to defend its privileged position, come what may. It enlists the

---

1 ibid., p. 124.

2 See Baran, *Political Economy*, pp. 219–271.

aid of religious prejudice and especially racial feeling to fight any group that bars the way to its own enrichment: 'The national bourgeoisie . . . which has totally assimilated colonialist thought in its most corrupt form, takes over from the Europeans and establishes in the continent a racial philosophy which is extremely harmful for the future of Africa'.[1] The post-colonial racism which is directed, e.g., against the Sudanese in Senegal, against Dahomeyans and immigrants from Upper Volta in the Ivory Coast, against Asian descendants in East Africa, against Negroes in Arab countries, and against Arabs in Black Africa, has its roots in the colonial period when minorities were often singled out and given privileged status. At the same time this development was given a further impetus by the fact that in many countries the entire trade was dominated by a minority, e.g., the Asians in East Africa; the Greeks and Lebanese in the Sudan; the Moabites in Algeria. The reasons for this can be found in the social structure of the countries concerned. If, for example, an ethnic group is ignorant of capital accumulation, its tradition has no place for a trading class. This enables an immigrant community to take over this function. After independence the bourgeoisie now tries to monopolize trade by means of racist propaganda. The loudly mouthed ideological formula of African unity only serves as a smokescreen to conceal the renewed flaring-up of old tribal feuds and religious bickering: 'From nationalism we have passed to ultra-nationalism, to chauvinism, and finally to racism'.[2]

Its feeling of insecurity and lack of a solid economic basis cause the national bourgeoisie to seek its salvation in the setting up of a one-party system: 'The single party is the modern form of the dictatorship of the

---

[1] Fanon, *The Wretched*, p. 131.
[2] ibid., p. 127.

bourgeoisie, unmasked, unpainted, unscrupulous, and cynical'.[1] It serves as an implement to gratify private lust for profit and as an instrument of power to control a population growing restless and dissatisfied. The party is headed by a charismatic leader who enjoys respect and prestige among the populace because of his role in the anticolonial struggle. 'The bourgeois dictatorship of underdeveloped countries draws its strength from the existence of a leader.'[2] Before independence, this patriot embodied the aspirations of the people; after independence he gradually becomes the accomplice of the corrupt bourgeoisie: 'He acts as a braking power on the awakening consciousness of the people. He comes to the aid of the bourgeois caste and hides his manoeuvres from the people, thus becoming the most eager worker in the task of mystifying and bewildering the masses'.[3] The army and the police, which are still under the supervision of foreign experts, support the regime. Should the control by the authoritarian unity party prove inadequate, the bourgeoisie secures its interests by means of a military dictatorship.

On the basis of his analysis Fanon comes to the conclusion that the developing countries do not necessarily have to go through a bourgeois phase as the economic structure of these countries differs from that

---

[1] ibid. p. 133. In contrast to this bourgeois dictatorship Fanon develops his own model of a decentralized unity party which should be an instrument in the hands of the people: 'For the people, the party is not an authority, but an organism through which they as the people exercise the authority and express their will'. (ibid., p. 149.) Party leadership and executive power are not to be identical, and a centralisation of the political leadership in the capital must be avoided at all costs. Instead, the hinterland must be given privileged status. The political enlightenment of the people is the precondition of the party's existence and at the same time its main task. Any economic, political and social measure taken by the government must be accompanied by a vast campaign of explanation: 'Everything can be explained to the people, on the single condition that you really want them to understand' (ibid., p. 151).

[2] ibid., p. 134.

[3] ibid., pp. 135–136.

of European societies during the early phase of industrialization: 'What creates a bourgeoisie is not the bourgeois spirit, nor its taste or manners, nor even its aspirations. The bourgeoisie is above all the direct product of precise economic conditions. Now, in the colonies, the economic conditions are conditions of a foreign bourgeoisie'.[1]

It is doubtless correct that both the bourgeoisie and the urban proletariat are coerced into an attitude of compromise from which the peasants by virtue of their objective position in the process of production are more or less immune. But it remains to be clarified in a number of concrete analyses pertaining to specific countries to what extent the peasants have actually been integrated into the social, i.e., colonial, production process. Peasants proletarianized by working in mines and plantations are bound to develop a revolutionary consciousness more easily than others growing cash crops on their own land, not to speak of those who have never abandoned their traditional way of life and who as subsistence farmers have never been immediately affected by the colonial production process. An analysis such as Fanon's, which shows a strong tendency to generalize, also leaves open the question whether revolutionary processes cannot after all be initiated among the proletariat with its much higher degree of organization: 'The working class in the colonies does not constitute a privileged class in the sense Fanon understands it, i.e., one pampered by the colonizers; rather it is privileged in the revolutionary sense of the word in so far as it is in the best position to watch the mechanisms of colonial exploitation at work at close

---

[1] ibid., p. 143.

quarters...'[1] Nguyen Nghe voices similar reservations—from the Vietnamese angle—with regard to Fanon's wholesale classification of the national bourgeoisie as a counter-revolutionary force: 'In colonized countries even the national bourgeoisie can, in spite of its flaws, participate in the revolution, including the building of socialism in one way or another'.[2]

Although Fanon's scheme of dividing colonial humanity into classes may justifiably be criticized as being too apodictal, there can be no question of the proletariat in the Third World playing a similar historical role as in Europe. In the colonial context the Marxian notion of the dictatorship of the proletariat has its counterpart in the theory of violence, a type of emancipatory counter-violence which is in the main practiced by the rural masses. Just as the Marxian notion defines revolutionary violence as counter-violence, thus a revolutionary theory of violence underpinning the liberation struggle must point out the requisite conditions for the abolition of violence. Fanon's theory meets this requirement only in an embryonic form.

Fanon's class analysis does not reflect the social and economic preconditions for emancipation in the countries of the so-called Third World. His analysis remains abstract; it is silent on the question of which functions in the process of emancipation could devolve upon individual groups in the colonial society under clearly defined conditions. A theory which wants to

---

[1] Nguyen Nghe, 'Frantz Fanon et les problemes de l'indépendance' in *La Pensée*, Paris, (February 1963): 29–31. Nghe's criticism of Fanon is an immanent one: he gauges his theory with reference to the experiences of the Vietnamese revolution. This should be compared with another Communist critic, Imre Marton, 'A propos des thèses de Fanon' in *Action*, no. 7–9, Fort-de-France, Martinique (1965), who in his dogmatic conceit and obviously without any knowledge of colonial problems is convinced that with some 'classical' Marxist-Leninist quotations he can disqualify Fanon as 'subjectivist'.

[2] ibid., p. 28.

fulfil these requirements must start from a concrete investigation of a given economic structure in relation to international forms of dependence. This will make it possible to determine the respective roles that can be played by the various social classes during and after the revolution, and what their political organization for achieving precisely defined aims (abolition of the international division of labour—realization of economic surplus by rationalizing agriculture—industrialization etc.) should be like. Only on the basis of such an analysis can it be further decided which socialization processes will guarantee a rapid economic growth combined with a minimum of repressive interiorization.

8. 'L'homme neuf': The Task of the Third World?

> The underdeveloped countries, which have used the fierce competition which exists between the two systems in order to assure the triumph of their struggle for national liberation, should however refuse to become a factor in that competition. The Third World ought not to be content to define itself in the terms of values which have preceded it. On the contrary, the underdeveloped countries ought to do their utmost to find their own particular values and methods and a style which shall be peculiar to them. The concrete problem we find ourselves up against is not that of a choice, cost what it may, between socialism and capitalism as they have been defined by men of other continents and other ages.[1]

FANON postulates the possibility of a 'third way' to development independent from the industrial nations, whether capitalist or socialist. In doing so he puts his trust in the revolutionary impact of awakening consciousness to such an extent that he fails to specify the economic conditions of such a development and to give any thought to the opposing forces which get mobilized at the slightest sign of incipient processes of liberation. His desperate rejection of Europe derives from his disappointment with the moral bankruptcy of the European working class movement, which itself benefited from colonialism instead of fighting the common exploiter in solidarity with the oppressed in the colonies. 'Any "yellow", "black" or differently

---

[1] Fanon, *The Wretched of the Earth*, trans. C. Farrington (London: MacGibbon & Kee, 1965), p. 78.

coloured "danger" provokes a solidarization effect which ranges from the big banks to the last trade union official. The internal class struggle grinds to a halt while the international one gains momentum.'[1] Fanon appeals to the exploited masses of the Third World finally to draw their consequences from the experiences undergone: 'Come, then, comrades, the European game has finally ended; we must find something different. We today can do everything, so long as we do not imitate Europe, so long as we are not obsessed by the desire to catch up with Europe...The Third World today faces Europe like a colossal mass whose aim should be to try to resolve the problems to which Europe has not been able to find the answers'.[2] The hope that the poor countries might achieve their liberation, which has always been the declared political aim of the European left although it has been belied by its actions, frequently emerges in discussions about the problems of the Third World. Is there a sizable chance for the economic basis of this liberation to be realized? Is it realistic to speak of the emergence of a 'new man' in the revolutionary countries of the Third World?

To answer this question, it has to be established whether there are any concrete indications that the colonial or semi-colonial territories will be capable of pursuing a path of industrialization which is substantially different both from capitalism and Soviet communism, which does not one-sidedly deform man in keeping with the requirements of the principles of reality and profitability in order to condition him for the production process: 'But let us be clear: what matters is to stop talking about output, and intensification, and the rhythm of work. No, there is no question

---

1 Hans Magnus Enzensberger, 'Europäische Peripherie', in *Kursbuch*, no. 2, Frankfurt u.M. (1966):163; cf. in this connection the controversy between Enzensberger and Peter Weiss, in *Kursbuch*, no. 6, Frankfurt a.M. (1966): 165–176.

2 Franon, *The Wretched*, pp. 252–254.

of a return to Nature. It is simply a very concrete question of not dragging men towards mutilation, of not imposing on the brain rhythms which very quickly obliterate it and wreck it'.[1] Herbert Marcuse is pessimistic in appraising the chances of a new form of industrialization capable of sustaining the Third World in its struggle for existence. Since the underdeveloped countries, in order to fend off any further exploitation by Western capitalism, are forced to abolish the pre-technological modes of production and industrialize their economies, they will of necessity have to pass through a stage of authoritarian administration which is bound to demand similar sacrifices as the industrialization of Europe: 'On the contrary, it rather seems that the superimposed development of these countries will bring about a period of total administration more violent and more rigid than that traversed by the advanced societies which can build on the achievements of the liberalistic era. To sum up: the backward areas are likely to succumb either to one of the various forms of neocolonialism, or to a more or less terroristic system of primary accumulation'.[2] However, Marcuse qualifies this statement by admitting a third possibility which would consist of making the pre-technological modes of life and labour themselves into the source of progress and industrialization; modern technology ought not to be superimposed on traditional modes of production but would have to extend and improve them on their own grounds: 'Self-determination would proceed from the base, and work for the necessities could transcend itself toward work for gratification'.[3]

---

[1] ibid., p. 254.

[2] Herbert Marcuse, *One-Dimensional Man* (London: Routledge and Kegan Paul, 1964), p. 47.

[3] ibid., p. 48. In presenting this model Marcuse surprisingly refers to the 'magnificent books' of René Dumont, whose analysis of Cuban development would rather seem to testify to the author's utter inability to understand the economic relevance of revolutionary political processes. R. Dumont, *Cuba—Socialisme et Devéloppement* (Paris: Editions du Seuil, 1964).

The term *Third World*, which is used in a generalizing fashion, has political and economic implications that are seldom clearly defined in the relevant discussions.[1] First it signified the young countries which after acceding to independence grouped themselves together as non-committed or neutral states to dissociate themselves from the existing power blocks. Their association corresponded to their need for political and national self-assertion after the period of colonial oppression. As a political designation for a large group of countries with heterogeneous economic and social structures, the term *Third World* does not, however, mean much. Although it is merely defined by a formal similarity of historical conditions—the end of colonialism—it intimates a common political and economic purpose which does not exist and thus contains an element of mystification rather than clarification.

With the repression of liberation movements by the imperialist powers entering its overt phase and the Vietnam war, which is symptomatic of this development, reaching its peak, the theory of the international class struggle, propounded mainly by the Chinese, has gained in importance both as a model to explain international forms of dependence and as a strategic concept for the liberation struggle of the underdeveloped countries. This model does not imply a tripartite world and three different paths to development but presupposes the alternative: socialism or capitalism, liberty or barbarity, in the name of which the poor, underdeveloped countries fight against the rich industrial nations. 'Let us take the whole world. If North America and Western Europe can be called the "cities of the world", Asia, Africa and Latin America

---

[1] *Third World* is often understood to mean a form of mixed economy in the developing countries which combines elements of a planned economy with those of a market economy, whereas the term is in the first place a political one.

can be termed "the world's rural areas"...In a certain sense the present world revolution offers a picture of the cities being encircled by the rural areas'.[1] According to this theory the increase and intensification of antagonism both among the imperialist countries and in their relations with the exploited masses of the poor world, lead to a permanent weakening of the imperialist system of authority. 'In this process the strength of the revolutionary movement in the colonies derives as much from the increasing social contradictions to the ruling classes in the imperialist countries as from the growing revolutionary consciousness of the peoples of the Third World themselves.'[2] The economic situation of the poor countries is bound to deteriorate in proportion as the general level of education and awareness keeps rising. As a result a revolutionary class consciousness will develop, and the class struggle will intensify. In the long run it will no longer be possible for the imperialist powers to curb this international trend with military force: 'The violent repression of national and social liberation movements is no longer practicable if it goes beyond the limited confines of a given territory and has to be carried out intensively on a global scale'.[3] At the same time these processes will intensify the class struggle in the highly industrialized countries and precipitate revolutionary conflicts. The struggles for liberation in the 'villages' of the world will not, however, automatically entail the fall of the 'cities': 'The mobilization and organization of the working classes of Western Europe will, however, be incumbent on the European socialists themselves. Even an "advanced Asia" can only facilitate the task of a backward Europe

---

1 Lin Piao, 'Es lebe der Sieg im Volkskrieg', in *Peking Rundschau*, 2nd year: no. 37 (1965): 26.

2 K. Steinhaus, *Zur Theorie des internationalen Klassenkampfes* (Frankfurt a.M.: Verlag neue Kritik, 1967), p. 16.

3 ibid., p. 45.

(Lenin); it cannot absolve her from her own responsibility'.[1]

Against the backdrop of this theory which is well-suited to give a more precise description of the economic conditions of emancipation than any vague formulations based on the notion of the *Third World*, one can now raise the problem of the 'new man'. Some elements of social reality are in fact a pointer to man's new possibilities: 'The reason why the former colonies and semi-colonies outside Europe have become the centres of violent social upheavals is in the first place that in those areas the "gulf...between the reasonable and the real" is often identical with that existing between safety and starvation and can therefore hardly be concealed by clever manipulations'.[2] The fact that men in the developing countries have not yet been deformed by the processes of repressive interiorization that characterize any phase of authoritarian industrialization offers them the chance of a new historical, more humane development. Whether the creation of the 'new man' is only possible on the basis of collective identification processes as intimated by Fanon's structuring of consciousness through violence, is a moot point. Che Guevara speaks of man's 'conscious, individual and collective participation in all the mechanisms of direction and production',[3] which in contrast to Fanon's theory, is, however, determined by concrete changes in the economic structure. The 'new man' is both a result and a pre-condition of the new society. 'There is still a long stretch to be covered in the construction of an economic base, and the temptation to take the beaten path of material interest as the lever of accelerated

1 ibid., p. 102.
2 K. Steinhaus, *Vietnam* (Frankfurt a.M.: Verlag neue Kritik, 1967), p. 38.
3 Ernesto Che Guevara, 'Socialism and Man in Cuba' (1965) in *Che, Selected Works of Ernesto Guevara* (Cambridge, Mass, and London: MIT Press, 1969), p. 162.

development is very great'.[1] The decisive factor in the process of emancipation is a constantly controlled interaction of the revolutionized social structures, norms and institutions on the one hand, and the individual's consciousness on the other: 'This is the indirect way of educating the masses...the process is a conscious one; the individual receives a continuous impact from the new social power and perceives that he is not completely adequate to it...What is important is that men acquire more awareness every day of the need to incorporate themselves into society, and, at the same time, of their importance as motors of that society.'[2]

---

[1] ibid., p. 159.
[2] ibid., pp. 160–161.

Bibliography

Adapted from the German edition and enlarged by Stella Ovbiagele Kragha, Assistant Librarian, University of Ife, Ile-Ife Nigeria.

A. Works by Fanon

BOOKS

Peau noire, masques blancs. Préface de Francis Jeanson. Paris: Editions du Seuil, 1952.

——**English editions**—*Black skin, white masks.* Trans. by Charles Lam Markmann. New York: Grove Press, 1965; London: Paladin, 1970.

L' An V de la Révolution Algérienne. Paris: Maspero, 1959. Later published as *Sociologie d'une revolution*. Paris: Maspero, 1966.

English editions—*Studies in a dying colonialism*, introduction by Adolfo Gilly. Trans. by Haakon Chevalier. New York: Monthly Review Press, 1965.

——*A dying colonialism*. New York: Grove Press, 1967; London: Penguin, 1970.

Les damnés de la terre. Préface de Jean Paul Sartre. Paris: Maspero, 1961, (Cahiers Libres Nos. 27/28); 1970 (Petite Collection Maspero 20).

——**English editions**—*The damned*. Trans. by Constance Farrington Paris: Présence Africaine, 1963.

——*The Wretched of the earth*. Trans. by Constance Farrington. New York: Grove Press, 1965, 1968; London: MacGibbon & Kee, 1965; Penguin, 1970.

Pour la Révolution Africaine, écrits politiques. Paris: Maspero, 1964 (Cahiers Libres Nos. 53/54).

English editions—*Toward the African revolution*. Trans. by Haakon Chevalier. New York: Monthly Review Press, 1967; New York: Grove Press, 1968; London: Penguin, 1970.

Note: This work contains most of the articles published in *El Moudjahid*. (See Section AII)

ARTICLES*

L'Expérience vécu du noir'. *Esprit,* Paris (May 1951).

'Le syndrome nord-africain,' *Esprit,* Paris, (Feb. 1952.)

'Sur quelques cas traités par la méthode de Bini,' (with F. Tosquelles, Saint Alban).
Congrès des médecins aliénistes et neurologues de France et des pays de langue française, LIe session, Pau, 20–26 Juillet 1953.

'A propos d'un cas de syndrome de Cotard avec balancenent psychosomatique'. (With M. Despinoy).

'Les Annales medico-psychologiques'. Tome 2, No. 2, Juin 1953 LIe session (Pau) 1953.

'Indications de thérapeutique de Bini dans le cadre des thérapeutiques institutionelles'. (With F. Tosquelles).
'*Congrès des médecins aliénistes et neurologues de France, et des pays de langue française,* LIe session'. Pau, 20–26 Juillet, 1953.

'Sur un essai de réadaptation chez une malade avec épilepsie morphéique et troubles des caractère grave'. (With F. Tosquelles).
'*Congrès des médecins aliénistes et neurologues de France et des pays de langue française,* LIe session'. Pau, Juillet 1953.

'Note sur les techniques des cures de sommeil avec conditionnement et contrôle électro-encéphalographique'. (With M Despinoy and W. Zenner).
'*Congrès des médecins aliénistes et neurologues de France et des pays de langue française,* LIe session'. Pau, 20–26 Juillet, 1953.

'La socialthéraphie dans un service d'hommes musulmans, difficultés méthodologiques, par les docteurs F. Fanon et J. Azoulay, Hôpital Psychiatrique de Blida-Joinville'. *L'Information Psychiatrique* 30me Année, 4me Série, 9, (1954) Paris.

'Introduction aux troubles de la sexualité chez les Nord-Africains'. (With J. Azoulay and F. Sanchez) Unpublished manuscript, about 1954/55.

'Aspects actuels de l'assistance mentale en Algérie'. (With J. Dequeker, R. Lacaton, M. Micucci, F. Rameé, Hôpital Psychiatrique de Blida-Joinville). *L'Information Psychiatrique* 31me Année, 4me Série 1 (1955) Paris.

'Antillais et Africains'. *Esprit* Paris (1955).

'Réflexions sur l'enthnopsychiatrie. *Conscience Maghrebine* 3, (1955)

'Conduites d'aveu en Afrique du Nord'. (With R. Lacaton) *Congrès des médecins aliénistes et neurologues de France et des pays de langue française, LIIIme session.* Nice, 5–11 September, 1955

* All asterisked articles are to be found in *Toward the African Revolution* (see section AI)

'Conférence sur les catégories de l'humanisme moderne' Unpublished lecture given at Blida, 1955.
'Attitude du musulman maghrebin devant la folie' (With F. Sanchez). *Revue pratique de psychologie de la vie sociale et d'hygiène mentale* 1 (1956)
'Lettre à un Français'. 1956.
'Lettre au Ministre Résidant'. 1956.
'Le T. A. T. chez la femme musulmane. Sociologie de la Perception et de l'Imagination', (With C. Geremini). *Congrès des médecines aliénistes et neurologues de France et des pays de langue française. LIVme session,* Bordeaux, 30 Août–4 Sept., 1956.
'Racisme et culture'. *Paper presented at the first Congress of Black Writers and Artists* Paris, September 1956.
'Le Phénomène de l'agitation en milieu psychiatrique. Considérations générales—signification psychopathologique', *Maroc Médical* (January 1957).
Press conference given in his capacity as speaker of the FLM in Tunis, *Le Monde* Paris, 5 June 1957.
'Déceptions et illusions du colonialisme français', *El Moudjahid* 10 (September 1957).
'L'Algérie face aux tortionnaires français', *El Moudjahid* 10 (September 1957).
'A propos d'un plaidoyer', *El Moudjahid,* 12 (November 1957).
'Les intellectuels et les démocrates français devant la révolution algérienne', *El Moudjahid,* 1, 15, 30 (December 1957).
'Aux Antilles, naissance d'une nation?', *El Moudjahid,* 16 (January 1958).
'A propos d'un cas de spasme de torsion' (With L. Levy). *La Tunisie Medicale* XXXVIme Année 9 (1958).
'Le sang maghrebin ne coulera pas en vain', *El Moudjahid,* 18 (February 1958).
'La farce qui change de camp', *El Moudjahid* 21 (April 1958).
'Décolonisation et indépendance', *El Moudjahid* 22 (April 1958).
'Une crise continuée', *El Moudjahid* 23 (May 1958).
'Lettre á la jeunesse africaine', *El Moudjahid* 24 (May 1958).
'Vérités premières à propos du problème colonial', *El Moudjahid* 24 (July 1958).
'La leçon de Cotonou', *El Moudjahid* 28 (August 1958)
'Appel aux Africains', *El Moudjahid* 29 (September 1958).
'Lendemains d'un plébiscite en Afrique', *El Moudjahid* 30, (Oct. 1958).
'La guerre d'Algérie et la libération des hommes', *El Moudjahid* 31 (November 1958).
'L'Algérie et Accra', *El Moudjahid* 34 (December 1958).

'Accra: l'Afrique affirme son unité et définit sa stratégie', *El Moudjahid* 34 (December 1958).

'Les tentatives désespérées de M. Debré', *El Moudjahid* 37 (Feb. 1959).

'Fureur raciste en France', *El Moudjahid* 42 (May 1959).

'Premiers essais de méprobamate injectable dans les états hypocondriaques' (With L. Levy) *La Tunisie Médicale* XXXVII me Année, Tunis (1959).

'L'hospitalisation de jour en psychiatrie, valeurs et limites, I. Introduction générale; II. Considérations doctrinales, (With C. Geromini.) *La Tunisie Médicale*, XXXVIIme Année, 10 Tunis (1959).

'Le sang coule aux Antilles sous domination française', *El Moudjahid* 58 (January 1960).

'Unité et solidarité effective sont les conditions de la libération africaine', *El Moudjahid* 58 (January 1960).

'Cette Afrique à venir'. 1960

Statement made at the Conference for Peace and Security in Africa. Accra, 7–10 April 1960; abridged version in *El Moudjahid* 63 (25 April 1960); full text in the second edition of *L'An V de la révolution algérienne*, but later omitted.

Statement made by Fanon as the Algerian representative at the Afro-Asian Conference held in Conakry, 12–15 April 1960; abridged version in *El Moudjahid* 63 (25 April 1960).

'The stages of imperialism', *Provisional Government of the Algerian Republic, Mission in Ghana* vol. 1, no. 6 (December 1960).

'La mort de Lumumba: Pouvions-nous faire autrement?', *Afrique Action* 19 (February 1961).

(iii) OTHER WORKS

Tam Tam 21 February 1948; edited by Fanon.

Les mains parallèles; L'oeil se noye; and *La conspiration*, 1949–50. (Three plays).

'Troubles mentaux et syndromes psychiatriques dans l'Hérédo-Dégénération-Spino-Cérébelleuse. Un cas de Maladie de Friedreich avec delire de possession', Lyon: Dissertation, 1951/52.

B. Works on Fanon

(i) BOOKS

Bouvier, Pierre. *Fanon* Paris: Editions universitaires, 1971.

Caute, David. *Frantz Fanon*. New York: Viking, London: Collins/ Fontana, 1970. 116pp.

Geismar, Peter. *Fanon.* New York: Dial Press, 1971. 214pp.

Gendzier, Irene L. *Frantz Fanon: a critical study.* New York: Pantheon, 1973. 300pp.

Lucas Philippe. *Sociologie de Frantz Fanon.* Algiers: SNED (Societé nationale d'edition ét de diffusion), 1971.

Zahar, Renate. *Kolonialismus und Entfremdung. Zur politischen Theorie Frantz Fanons.* Frankfurt am Main: Europäische Verlagsanstalt, 1959, 115pp.

French edition—*L'oeuvre de Frantz Fanon.* Trans. by Roger Dangeville. Petite Collection Maspero, No. 57. Paris: Maspero, 1970. 127pp.

(ii) ARTICLES, PASSAGES AND ESSAYS IN BOOKS

Jahn, Janheinz. *A history of neo-African literature.* Trans. from German by Oliver Coburn and Ursula Lehrburger. London: Faber, 1966; New York: Grove Press, 1969. pp. 277–282.

Jeanson, Francis. Préface, *Peau noire, masques blancs.* Paris: 1952.

——'Reconnaissance de Fanon', postface, *Peau noire masques blancs.* Paris: 1965.

Mainberger, Gonsalv. 'Frantz Fanon: the myth and reality of the Negro'. In *Black Leaders of the Centuries.* Ed. by S. O. Mezu and R. Desai. Buffalo, New York: Black Academy Press, 1970, pp. 267–279.

Pirelli, Giovanni. Introduction, *L' An V de la révolution algérienne.* (Italian ed.) Turin: 1963.

Sartre, Jean Paul. Preface, *Les damnés de la terre.* Paris: 1961. Also published in *Situations V*, Paris: 1964.

Wallerstein, Immanuel. 'Frantz Fanon', In *International Encyclopaedia of the Social Sciences.* Ed. by David L. Sille. New York: Macmillan and the Free Press, 1968. Vol. 5, pp. 326–7.

(iii) ARTICLES IN JOURNALS

Abel, Lionel. Seven heroes of the new Left', *New York Times Magazine* (5 May 1968): 30–31.

Abrash, Barbara. 'Frantz Fanon: bio-bibliography', *Africana Library Journal*, II, 3 (Autumn 1971).

——'Frantz Fanon as Mythmaker', Conference of the African Studies Association, Philadelphia, November 1972.

Ansprenger, Franz. 'A review of *Les damnés de la terre*', *J. of Modern African Studies* (London), I, 3 (1963)

Arendt, Hannah. 'Reflections on violence', *New York Review of Books*, 12, 4 (27 February 1968): 19–31.

Barnard, Roger. 'Frantz Fanon', *New Society* 275 (4 January 1968) : 11–13.

Beckett, P. A. 'Frantz Fanon and sub-Saharan Africa: notes on the contemporary significance of his thought', *Africa Today* 19, 2 (Spring 1972): 59–72.

Bondy, François. 'The black Rousseau', *The New York Review*, 3 March 1966.

Bourgui A. C. and Williams J.—C. 'La pensée politique de Frantz Fanon', *Présence Africaine* (Paris) N.B.S. 88 (4th Quarterly 1973): 137–162.

——'Anwalt der Verdammten', *Der Monat*, (Berlin) August 1966.

Brown, Phil. 'Notes on Fanon', *The Radical Therapist* (Minor, North Dakota) I, 19 (1970): 11.

Capoçye, Emile. 'Time to turn a tide of violence?' *Saturday Review* (New York) 24 April 1965.

Case, F. I. 'Aimé Césaire et Frantz Fanon', Théoricien de la litérature révolutionaire, Conference of the Modern Language Association, New York, December 1972.

Caute, David. 'Philosopher of violence', *The Observer*, (London) 10 October 1965.

Cherif, Mohammed. 'La science au service de la révolution' *Jeune Afrique* (Paris) 295 (1966).

Clark, Richard C. 'Contrasting views of "Black" African literature *Review of National Literature*, 2, 2 (Fall 1971), special issue on *Black Africa* New York: St. John's University Press, 1972.

Coles, Robert. 'What colonialism does', *The New Republic*, 9 August 1965.

Colotti-Pischel, Enrica. 'Fanonismo e questione coloniale', *Problemi del Socialismo*, (Milano) September/October 1962.

Coser, Lewis. 'The myth of peasant revolt', *Dissent* (New York) May/June 1966.

Cruise O'Brien, Conor. 'The neurosis of colonialism', *The Nation*, 21 June 1965.

Domenach, Jean-Marie. 'Sur une préface de Jean-Paul Sartre', *Esprit*, (Paris) March 1962.

——A review of *Les damnés de la terre*. *Esprit* (Paris) April 1962.

——'Critique et réponse de Domenach', *Esprit* (Paris) September 1962.

Dubois, François. A review of *Pour la révolution africaine*, *Tiers Monde* (Paris) 19, V (1964).

Fornari, Franco. 'Violenza e colpa', *Aut-Aut* (Milan) 74/75 (1963)

Forsythe, Dennis. 'Frantz Fanon: black theoretician', *The Black Scholar* San Francisco I, 5 (March 1970): 2–10.

Garrett, Jan. 'A review', *Young Socialist* (New York) November/December 1965.

Geismar, Peter and Worseley, Peter. 'Frantz Fanon: evolution of a revolutionary', *Monthly Review* New York 21, 1 (May 1969) 22–49.

Gendzier, Irene L. 'Frantz Fanon: in search of justice', *Middle East Journal* (1966).

——Frantz Fanon: 'From Psychiatry to Political Action', Conference of the African Studies Association, Philadelphia, November 1972.

Gilly, Adolfo 'Frantz Fanon et la révolution en Amérique Latine', *Partisans* (Paris, 21 (1965).

Giudici, Giovanni. 'Fanon e noi', *Quaderni Piacentini*, (Piacenza) September/October 1963.

Gleason, Ralph. 'An introduction to Frantz Fanon', *Ramparts*, March 1966.

Gramont, S. de. 'Frantz Fanon: the prophet scorned', *Horizon* 14 (Winter 1972): 32–7.

Gottheil, F. M. 'Fanon and the economics of colonialism', *Review of Economics and Business*, 7, 3 (Autumn, 1967).

Grohs, G. K. Frantz 'Fanon, ein Theoretiker der afrikanischen Revolution', *Kölner Zeitschrift für Soziologie und Sozialpsychologie*, Köln und Opladen 16, 3 (1964)

——'Frantz Fanon and the African revolution', *J. of Modern African Studies*, 6, 4 (December 1968): 543–556.

Haag, Ernest van den. 'On torture', *Modern Age* (Spring 1966).

Hale, Dennis. A review. *Motive*: (January 1966).

Hamdani, Hassan. 'La pensée révolutionnaire de Frantz Fanon', *Révolution Africaine*, Alger 71/72.

Hansen, Emmanuel. 'Frantz Fanon: A Bibliographical Essay', Conference of the African Studies Association, Philadelphia, November 1972.

Hanthoff, Nat. 'Bursting into history', *The New Yorker*, 15 Jan. 1966.

Hermassi, Abdelbaki. 'L'idéologie fanonienne', *Jeune Afrique* Tunis, 295 (September 1966).

Hoechstetter, Irene. 'L'homme de la décolonisation', *Réforme*, (December 1966).

'Homage to Frantz Fanon', *Présence Africaine*, 40 (Eng. ed. vol. 12, pp. 130–152; French ed. pp. 118–141) 1962. (10 messages from writers, politicians and scholars on Fanon's death—Césaire, Maspero, Nkrumah and others).

Isaacs, Harold R. 'Portrait of a revolutionary', *Commentary*, 40, 1 (July 1966): 67–71.

Jaeggi, Urs. 'Gewalt und Gegenwalt', *Züricher Weltwoche*, 23 December 1966.

Jones, John Henry. 'On the influence of Fanon', *Freedomways* 8, 3 (Summer 1968): 209–214.

Judson, Horace. 'Master and Slave: a review of Irene L. Gendzier's *Frantz Fanon: a critical study*', *Time* 2 April 1973: 63–64.

Kaufmann, Herbert. 'Hilft nur noch Gewalt?' *Der Spiegel*, Hamburg 1 August 1966.

Kershaw, Richard. 'Manifesto of rebellion, *Sunday Times*, London 10 October 1965.

King, Slater. 'The Wretched of the Earth are here too', *Monthly Review*, New York 18, 2 (1966).

Klein, Norman A. 'On revolutionary violence', *Studies on the Left* New York 6, 3 (1966).

Lacouture, Jean. Two lectures given at the Ecole Nationale d'Administration, Paris, 1963, (unpublished manuscripts), 'L'oeuvre de Frantz Fanon' and 'Frantz Fanon et notre temps'.

——'A review of *Les damnés de la terre*', *Le Monde*, Paris 23 February 1962.

Lomax, L. A. 'Martyr to hope', *The Tribune* London (May 1965).

London, Perry. 'Multi-faced treatise on colonial revolution', *Los Angeles Times*, 23 May 1965.

Malabre, Alfred L. 'A disturbing diatribe from the Third World,' *Wall Street Journal*, New York 23 July 1965.

Maldonado Denis, M. 'Frantz Fanon (1924–1961) y el pensamiento anticolonialista contemporáneo', (Frantz Fanon and contemporary anticolonialist thought). *Revista de Ciencias Sociales* Puerto Rico: II, 1 (March 1967): 55–69.

Martin, T. 'Rescuing Fanon from the critics', *African Studies Review*, 13, 3 December 1970: 381–399.

Marton, Imre. A propos des théses de Fanon: (l) Le rôle de la violence dans la lutte de libération nationale, (2) Le rôle des classes sociales après l'indépendance. *Action* Fort-de France, Martinque 7, 8, 9 (1965)

Maschino, Maurice. 'Frantz Fanon, l'itinéraire de la générosité, *Partisans* Paris 3 (1962).

——'A review of *L'An de la Révolution Algérienne*' *Les Temps Modernes* Paris 167/168 (1960).

Mintz, Donald. 'Find something different,' *Washington Evening Star*, 21 March 1965

Nghe, Nguyen. 'Frantz Fanon et les problèmes de l'indépendance *Le Pensée* Paris 107 (February 1962).

Ngnepi, Guillaume-Henri. 'Aspects de la culture chez Frantz Fanon', *L'Ecriture* (Editions CLE, Yaoundé, Cameroun), 4 Decembre 1973: 15–22

Nursey-Bray, P. 'Marxism and Existentialism in the thought of Frantz Fanon', *Political Studies* 20 (June 1972): 152–168.

Olaniyan, Richard. 'Fanon revisited: a review of I.L. Gendzier's *Frantz Fanon: a critical study*', *Sunday Times* (Lagos, Nigeria) 13 May 1973: 17.

Pable, M. '*Les damnés de la terre: a review*', *Quatrième Internationale* 15 (1962).

Paris, Robert. 'Sur un premier bilan du "fanonisme"', *Partisans* Paris 8 (1963).

Perinbaum, B. Marie. 'Fanon and the revolutionary peasantry: the Algerian case,' *Journal of Modern African Studies* II (September) 1970: 427–445.

Posinsky, S. H. 'A review,' *Psychoanalytical Quarterly* New York 35, 4.

Pouillon, Jean. 'Décolonisation et révolution', *Les Temps Modernes* Paris, 191 (1962).

Quellel, Charif. 'Frantz Fanon and colonised man', *Africa Today* 17, (January/February 1970): 8–12.

Ranly, Ernest W. 'Frantz Fanon and the radical left', *America* 121, 14 (1 November 1969) 384,: 387, 388.

Rohdie, Samuel. 'Liberation and violence in Algeria', *Studies on the Left* New York 6, 3 (May/June 1966).

Schuon, Karl Theodor. 'Fanons Lehre von der befreienden Gewalt', *Das Argument* Jhrg. 45, 9 (December 1967).

Seigel, J. E. 'On Frantz Fanon', *American Scholar* 38, 1 (Winter 1968): 84–96.

Solodkin, P. '*Fanon*, by P. Geismar: a review' *Catholic World*, 214 (November 1971) 86–7.

Stambouli, F. 'Frantz Fanon face aux problèmes de la décolonisation et de la construction nationale', *Revue de l'Institut de Sociologie* Bruxelles 2/3 (1967) 519–534.

Staniland, Martin. Frantz Fanon and the African political class', *African Affairs*, 68, 270 (January 1968): 4–25.

Stetler, Russ. 'The works of Frantz Fanon', *Liberation U.S.A.*, 10.

Sutton, H. 'Fanon', *Saturday Review*, 54 (17 July 1971): 16–19.

Tibi, Bassam. 'Frantz Fanons Gewalttheorie in Zusammenhang mit seiner Hegel-Rezeption', (unpublished manuscript) 1969

Vetter, Hans. 'Lehrbuch und Manifest für alle, die getreten werden', *Kölner Stadtanzeiger* (Cologne) 14 January 1967.

Worseley, Peter. 'The coming inheritors', *The Guardian* (Manchester) 22 October 1965.

Zahar, Renate. 'Frantz Fanons anti-kolonialistisches Manifest', *Neue Kritik* 38/39 (1966).
Zehm, Günter. 'Zurück in den Urwald?' *Die Welt*, (Hamburg) 27 August 1966.
Zolberg, Aristide R. 'Frantz Fanon: a gospel for the damned', *Encounter* 27 (November 1966): 56–63.
——'The Americanisation of Frantz Fanon', *The Public Interest*, 9 (1967).

ANONYMOUS ARTICLES

'Prisoner of hate', *Time* (New York) 30 April 1965.
'Das Strip-tease unseres Humanismus', *Süddeutsche Zeitung* (München) 13 August 1966.
'Europa hat ausgespielt', *Die Zeit* (*Hamburg*) 23 Sept. 1966.
'Ein böses Buch—ein gutes Buch', *Frankfurter Allgemeine Zeitung* (Frankfurt) 11 October 1966.
Plädoyer für die Entrechteten', *Die andere Zeitung* (Hamburg) 27 October 1966.
'Die Verdammten dieser Erde', *Vorwärts* (Bad Godesberg) 19 January 1967
'Camus and some others. Portrait', *Times Literary Supplement*, (London) 69, 29 January 1970: 97–8.